TUNNEL VISION

A True Story of Multiple Murder
and Justice in Chaos
at America's Biggest Marine Base

N.P. SIMPSON

 Down Home Press, Asheboro, N.C.

ISBN No. 1-878086-24-3

Library of Congress Catalog Card Number
93-071405

Printed in the United States of America

Cover design: Tim Rickard
Book design: Elizabeth House

Down Home Press
P.O. Box 4126
Asheboro, N.C. 27204

ACKNOWLEDGEMENTS

This book began at a Boys and Girls Club board meeting in Jacksonville, N.C., where I mentioned to Chairman Chuck Henry that I was interested in writing a book about the murder of a young couple that happened in 1990.

Chuck agreed that the case would make an intriguing book but added, "Now, the case I think would make a really interesting book is the Butch Smith case." I had heard of Butch Smith but was not aware that Chuck had been one of Butch's attorneys.

It was an opportunity that I could not let pass. To clear the legal path, Chuck acted as intermediary between Butch, his mother and me. Butch agreed to release Chuck from privilege and release me from liability.

At no time did Butch or his mother ask for or receive any consideration for these releases. Nor did they try to influence my account of events.

Because Chuck Henry, with Butch's consent, gave me the material he had obtained through discovery, I had access to witness statements, autopsy reports, psychiatric records and court transcripts I would not have been able to get otherwise.

I am very grateful for Chuck's encouragement and unfailing enthusiasm for the project.

The other lawyers concerned in the case, the two prosecutors as well as Butch's other attorney, Rick Cannon, also were helpful, courteous and wonderfully outspoken.

It was a great asset to be allowed use of *Jacksonville Daily News* facilities. I thank editor Elliott Potter for the privilege. Also especially helpful were office manager Mary Jo Hamrick and photographer Randy Davey.

I thank the NIS agents, former and present, who spoke to me so candidly. I was impressed by their zeal and their idealism. Some names in this book have been changed to protect privacy. Those changed are indicated with an asterisk on first use.

CONTENTS

CHAPTER 1

ONTARIO, OREGON

1986

The Oregon border town of Ontario seems an improbable setting for a cluster of military recruiting offices. Its residents number fewer than 10,000. That's not likely to change much. There's no industry and little else to entice job seekers from elsewhere.

Even the area's climate is more detriment than lure. Stovehouse summers and deep-freeze winters are typical of eastern Oregon's Columbia Plateau. The brittle beauty of its high desert is untempered by the Pacific winds that gentle the state's coastal weather.

Most nineteenth-century homesteaders pressed on toward the lushly forested western part of the state. Latter-day tourists are likely to do the same. But visitors from surrounding smaller towns bring more bustle and business to Ontario than its own population would indicate. And the lack of a state sales tax in Oregon lures many shoppers from nearby Idaho.

Staff Sgt. Kevin McMorris* liked Ontario just fine. He was convinced his job as a recruiter for the Oregon Army National Guard was a plum worth preserving. And Ontario's unsparing climate didn't faze the native Northwesterner.

He, like all National Guard recruiters, was part of the Active Guard Reserve. AGR members serve full-time. Unlike recruiters from other branches of the military, National Guard recruiters are not subject to the routine three-year rotations that shift most soldiers and sailors from one duty station to another. McMorris had been a recruiter for two years.

On March 15, 1986, a young man McMorris later recalled as slender and clean-cut came into the recruiting office. He was accompanied by his mother, a petite, friendly woman with a ready smile.

After some general discussion of the National Guard, the young man, who identified himself as Butch Smith, age 20, said he wished to join as soon as possible. The woman, Betty Francis, dominated the conversation, McMorris recalled. The quiet youth appeared nervous.

"He really didn't want to look at me," McMorris recalled. But McMorris did not think the young man's nervousness was particularly unusual. Nor was it unusual for a parent to assume the upper hand during discussions with a recruiter.

"The hardest part of being a recruiter is living down the reputation of promising anything just to get a recruit. Parents want to be sure their son isn't railroaded," McMorris explained.

Smith began to fill out application papers while his mother looked on. McMorris noticed that Smith appeared to have difficulty with one of the questions and turned to his mother for advice. McMorris asked what the problem was.

Smith said one of the questions asked if the applicant had ever been in a mental institution.

"I have been," he told McMorris.

The woman quickly admonished her son, "Why did you tell him that? You shouldn't have."

Her response alerted McMorris. He reminded her that the questions must be answered honestly. He added that a person

2

was not necessarily disqualified from service because he had been in a mental institution. Perhaps, there were extenuating circumstances. It was necessary to know why the person was in the institution.

The youth told McMorris it was because of the death of his sister.

His mother explained that her son had been in an institution for evaluation because his sister had been murdered at Camp Lejeune in North Carolina five years earlier. She said her son, who had been in the house at the time, had taken the death very hard and had been hospitalized for observation.

McMorris nodded sympathetically. That was a prime example of the kind of extenuating circumstances he had referred to, he said. "Chances are, a person needs counseling if they go through something like that," he told the woman.

However, McMorris gently persisted, it would be necessary for him to get a copy of Smith's treatment record from the hospital.

His mother shook her head. That would be impossible, she said, because the murder had not been solved. Camp Lejeune would not release the records.

McMorris assured her if proper procedures were followed, the Marine base would release pertinent records to a recruiter.

The woman hesitated a moment before responding. "Well, it goes a little bit further than that," she said. "He's a suspect."

"A suspect?"

"Yes. He hasn't been charged. The reason he's a suspect is because he was in the house."

"That's the only reason?"

"Yes."

McMorris did not ask for details of the unusual revelations. He did tell the woman that it would be nonetheless necessary that he see Smith's medical evaluation.

Betty Francis offered to call the Naval Investigative Service at Camp Lejeune from McMorris' office. NIS is the civil service organization responsible for criminal investigations on Navy and Marine Corps bases. She telephoned Camp Lejeune, spoke briefly to an NIS agent then passed the telephone to McMorris. The agent to whom McMorris spoke explained the procedures the recruiter must follow to get Smith's records.

Their conversation took an ominous turn when the agent told the recruiter that once McMorris reviewed the young man's records, he probably would not wish to enlist Smith.

After the phone call, McMorris told Betty Francis that her son's enlistment was "on ice" until he could go over the medical report. Mother and son then left the recruiter's office.

Within the hour, an NIS agent called McMorris and told him they had been looking for Smith for some time. They wanted more information in order to continue the investigation. The agent told the recruiter that plans already were under way for NIS agents to visit Oregon in order to interview McMorris and Smith.

During the following weeks, while McMorris awaited the medical report, Butch Smith telephoned several times to track the progress of his enlistment effort. In late April, Smith stopped by McMorris' office. He seemed more at ease than when he had been with his mother, McMorris recalled.

The recruiter and the sandy-haired young man discussed several things. Smith expressed great interest in military matters. Curious, McMorris brought up the subject of Smith's being a suspect in the death of his sister.

Smith told McMorris that he and a friend had been fishing the day of the murder and had returned home at about 1:00 a.m. He said that he and his friend had gone to sleep in the same room and awakened between 6:00 and 7:00 the next morning.

"Then the nightmare started."

He heard a muffled scream, he continued, and went to load his shotgun. He woke two other boys. "Come with me," he told them. "We got real problems."

Smith said the three boys discovered three murder victims, including Smith's sister, his cousin and another person. One of the boys ran out of the house screaming because the third victim was his mother, Smith said. Smith said he had gone to a neighbor's house to call the police.

Why did police suspect him? McMorris asked.

"Because it was my fishing knife that was used to kill them." He said he had left the knife in the garage after returning from fishing.

It also was because a psychiatrist had asked him to speculate, "If you were going to kill someone, how would you do it?"

Smith said he told the doctor, "I would sneak up behind them and hold my hand in front of their face, and stab them in the side of the throat putting the blade into their voice box, then bring the knife over to the center of the throat and pull down hard towards the center of the ribs."

What he had described, Smith said, was the manner in which the victims actually were slain. His father had told him that was how they were killed, he said.

Was he having problems with his sister? McMorris asked.

No. He had loved her very much. If he found out who had killed her, he added, he would kill that person.

As the recruiter had listened to Smith's account of these grisly events, the psychiatric report he was awaiting took on greater significance.

"Running through my mind was that he was a very disturbed little boy. And he needed some help," McMorris later recalled.

What McMorris did not know was that he was one of many who had either already described Smith as disturbed or would do so in years to come.

And Smith's account of the night his sister died was only one of many he had already told – and would tell in years to come.

And none of Smith's accounts, including a confession, would agree with the testimony of others or explain evidence found at the scene.

CHAPTER 2

CAMP LEJEUNE
MONDAY, AUGUST 24, 1981

A feverish affliction of heat and humidity settles on coastal North Carolina during August.

Families of Marines stationed at Camp Lejeune eagerly wait for their names to reach the top of the base housing list. In base quarters they may enjoy the comfort of air conditioning without the burden of attendant electric bills.

It is not true that service members get "free" housing. A quarters allowance included in their paychecks while they live off-base is deducted when the military family moves into base housing. But, especially for enlisted families, base housing is often roomier and more attractive than the trailer parks and apartment complexes available off-base for the same price. And base housing residents are not billed separately for utilities and maintenance.

Watkins Village is a 250-unit housing area reserved for the families of married corporals, sergeants and staff sergeants.

Two-story duplexes with adjoining garages are grouped along streets and circular courts named for states.

Playgrounds and tennis courts are part of the layout, which backs up to a wooded area.

In some respects, Watkins is actually several small neighborhoods bumping up against each other.

"In some areas, everybody's nosy and everybody knows each other. In other areas, every kid looks alike," one resident explained.

On one side of Watkins Village are the base stables, where Shetland ponies plod around a ring carrying delighted toddlers. More affluent equestrians may board their own horses and take lessons on either English or western saddles.

On the other side of Watkins Village is Berkley Manor, an area of single-family ranch houses reserved for senior enlisted Marines, including gunnery sergeants, master sergeants and sergeants major. The shared entrance to the two NCO housing areas intersects with the more heavily traveled Stone Street. A convenience store on the corner is a popular stop for residents in need of a can of baby formula or a pack of cigarettes. Youngsters passing to and from the base schools on Stone Street stop at the store to buy jawbreakers and ice cream sandwiches.

The day begins early at a Marine base. At 7:00 a.m., August 24, 1981, the Stone Street store was already open. A young Marine on his way to work honked his car horn and startled the sleepy female clerk sweeping up a broken bottle in the parking lot.

Inside, a woman Marine in utilities bought a *Navy Times* and a box of powdered-sugar doughnuts. She and a freckle-faced lance corporal commented on the quirks of the weather and the new company commander.

A construction worker, part of the crew building the new naval hospital, bought a vacuum-sealed package of beef jerky.

Several rainstorms during the past week had tempered the heat to the mid-80s. Sunday's cloudiness, predicted to continue through the beginning of the week, also had honed some of the edge off August's typically brutal heat.

Nearby, in the duplex at 1080A Kentucky Court 12-year-old Tommy Sager was just waking up. Although he'd stayed up past midnight, he was nudged from sleep by a pressing need to use the bathroom.

The boy was in the top of bunk beds he shared with his 15-year-old cousin, Butch Smith. Butch was still asleep, his fists tucked under his chin. Because of his deep-set eyes and merging eyebrows, Butch looked as if he were scowling even when he was asleep.

Tommy, his stepmother and five brothers and sisters had been staying at Camp Lejeune with the Smith family since early August. Tommy's stepmother, Sharon, and Butch's mother, Betty, were sisters.

Tommy's father, a sergeant in the Army, was en route to a new duty station in Alaska. When he had found them a place to live, he was to send for his family.

Saturday, the cousins and aunts had returned from a trip to New York, where they had stayed with Sharon's and Betty's parents – Butch's grandparents.

Tommy untangled the sheet and let his legs flop over the side of the bed. He had slept soundly. He had not been disturbed by the noise of the television downstairs or the other siblings and cousins still up when he went to bed.

Deaf in one ear, Tommy heard very little if he slept on his good ear. Anyway, the central air conditioning tended to drown out sounds from downstairs and the other rooms upstairs when the door was closed.

As he was about to swing down to the floor, Tommy remembered the toy pellet gun and bag of green, pea-sized ammunition he had stashed under his pillow the night before. His mother had bought Tommy, his two brothers, Chris and Tyler, and his cousin Butch pellet guns during a Sunday shopping trip. The boys had spent much of the evening before gleefully shooting at a variety of targets, including each other.

The need to get to the bathroom became secondary.

Tommy patted the bedclothes in search of his pellet gun. When he could not find it, he hopped down from the top bunk and gingerly slipped his hand under Butch's pillow. The older boy mumbled but did not stir during his cousin's fruitless hunt.

Tommy glanced at the jeans and shirt Butch had stripped off and dropped on the floor before going to bed. He spotted one of the toy guns on a chair. But it was not his.

The boy then went out the open door and into the adjacent bedroom where his brother, Chris, 13, was sleeping.

The room was really his cousin Connie's room. Connie was Butch's sister. But Connie and Butch's other sister, Lorrie, and Tommy's stepsister, Debbie, had decided to spend the night in the family's red station wagon. The vehicle was parked outside the duplex front door, directly beneath the window of the room where Chris was asleep.

Tommy still couldn't find his gun so he crossed the hall to Lorrie's room. The door was partly open when he pushed on it. He got no further than the threshold before he was overwhelmed by a rush of horror.

Tommy's stepbrother Tyler lay on a blood-soaked bed, his shirt awash in dark red. Blood from his ear trailed into a pool that haloed his neck and head.

For a moment, Tommy was immobilized, trying to sort out whether he was truly seeing what he thought he was seeing. Then he jerked around and raced back across the hall to the room where Butch was still asleep.

"Tyler's dead! Tyler's dead! In Lorrie's room!" Tommy shouted as he shook his cousin.

"Leave me alone, will ya" Butch growled.

"There's blood all over!" Tommy sobbed, desperately trying to pull the older boy out of bed.

"Ah, it's probably just some trick Tyler and Chris are pulling," Butch said as he got up. The boys had pulled pranks on each other before. But the urgency and alarm in Tommy's voice spurred Butch to hurry into the room across the hall.

Tyler was facing the wall with his arms flung back above his head. Butch touched Tyler's shoulder.

"Tyler," he said. "Tyler."

Tyler's head suddenly lolled backward and Butch glimpsed the glistening, gaping wound angled deeply into the left side of his cousin's throat.

9

Butch later would tell investigators that he grasped Tyler's upturned wrist, seeking a pulse. Butch's mother was a nurse. She had drilled her children on first-aid procedures since they were small.

Butch fled the room with Tommy close behind. He returned to his own room and pulled on his pants.

Tommy alerted Chris, who was now also aware that Tyler probably was dead. They were uncertain what to do. Investigators later would ask Butch why neither he nor his cousins yelled for help. It was only one of many unanswerable questions the day would present.

The three boys went downstairs, turned right and ran down the hall toward the playroom at the rear of the duplex. They knew that Sharon Sager, Butch's aunt as well as Chris and Tommy's stepmother, had spent the night on a couch in the playroom. Butch's mother, Elizabeth Smith, called Betty, had not been home the night before. His Aunt Sharon had been the only adult in the house.

The playroom couch was clearly visible from the hallway. There was no door between the playroom and the hall. Only a serving counter separated the kitchen from the playroom. The drapes over the playroom window and the patio door were closed. Except for faint spill-over illumination from the stove light and break-through glimmers of morning sunshine, the playroom was dark.

Across the room from where Sharon Sager lay motionless, four couch cushions had been arranged on the floor to serve as a makeshift bed. Three small boys, Scotty and Skippy Sager and a neighbor child, Bobby Davis, were curled up on the cushions, scarcely visible in the gloom. They were less than 10 feet from the couch where Skippy and Scotty's mother lay.

Butch flipped the light switch and then recoiled toward the doorway where Chris and Tommy stood close together.

Sharon Sager would not be able to advise them about Tyler. She, too, lay in blood-soaked disarray. Her face, except for the wide-open hazel eyes, was a smear of red. The front of her nylon nightgown was the same garish red as Tyler's shirt. Deep wounds had partially severed her head from her body.

Butch stumbled backward, wheeled and raced toward the front door, his cousins at his heels. In their fright, they did not stop to check the three small children who lay unmoving in the shadows.

Chris and Tommy banged on the windows of the red station wagon to alert the three girls thought to be inside. Butch ran to the nearest neighbor's house and pounded on the door. There was no answer.

He did not go to the door of the duplex attached to the Smith quarters. He knew that those residents were away on vacation. Instead, he ran behind the duplex and sought help from another neighbor who had no phone. Butch then went to a third house. The door was answered by Harold Rodriguez.* Rodriguez' wife, Susan*, was a friend of Butch's mother. Rodriguez had been awakened by the loud banging at the door.

"Can you call the MPs?" Butch asked breathlessly.

Susan Rodriguez, who had followed her husband to the door, thought the boy was joking.

"Now, why do you want to call the MPs, Butch?"

"My family's been murdered," Butch blurted out.

Susan drew the distraught boy into the house. Her husband looked from the boy's ashen face to his wife's astounded one and quickly headed toward the Smith house.

Susan called the MPs. They asked to speak to Butch. He repeated that there had been a murder at his house. After he hung up, Susan asked Butch where his sisters, Connie and Lorrie, were. Butch said he didn't know.

He tried to explain the previous hour's events, how he and Tommy and Chris had found the bodies of Tyler and Sharon Sager.

"There was blood all over both of them," Butch told her. He gnawed at fingernails that were already chewed well short of the tips of his fingers. Susan noticed a plastic bandage strip on Butch's wrist.

She and Butch went to the front porch of her duplex and saw that a crowd was gathering around the Smith house. Butch became extremely upset at this, Susan later told investigators. He shouted at the onlookers, telling them to leave. She gently guided Butch back inside to wait for her husband and a military policeman to join them.

While they waited, Susan fetched a clean white T-shirt for Butch to put on. He was shaking convulsively.

Lorrie Smith, 13, was curled up asleep in the back seat of her Aunt Sharon's station wagon. Her cousin Deborah, 12, was next to her, their heads nearly touching. Scattered on the floorboard were the cards they had been playing with the night before and empty cellophane snack-food bags. The car was parked with its rear bumper within a few feet of the front door to the Smith's quarters.

Sleeping in the car was something of an adventure for the girls. They had planned to do it Saturday night, when Butch's friend, Tom Cheek, had swelled the number of youngsters staying in the Smith household to 10. But the girls changed their minds when several vehicles they didn't recognize turned the court into a circular drag strip.

When Lorrie's mother had called from a friend's house at 11:00 the night before, Lorrie had asked permission to sleep in the car because the boys were making so much noise in the house. Her mother admitted there was quite a din in the background but she didn't want the girls to sleep outside.

Lorrie and Connie had already wheedled permission from their Aunt Sharon, who was babysitting in Betty Smith's absence. The girls seemed so excited about the prospect of camping out in the car that Betty relented.

Connie Smith, 12, had intended to spend the whole night in the car with her sister and her cousin. But at about 4:00 a.m., Lorrie and Debbie were awakened when they heard Connie open the car door to go inside.

Connie was a sweet-faced blond, still more child than adolescent. Sensitive about being overweight and having a back condition that forced her to walk with a slightly impaired gait, Connie was nonetheless a strikingly pretty girl. She was chilly and uncomfortable, she told the other girls. She had decided to go inside and sleep on the couch in the living room.

It was not unusual for Connie to sleep on the living room couch and wait for her mother to return from socializing or a late shift at the nursing home where she worked.

The living room was to the right of the duplex's front hallway. The couch, flush against the east wall, served as a divider between the living room and the dining room.

Tall and slender, Lorrie, 13, seemed more than a year older than her sister. Like many big sisters, she fancied herself much more sophisticated than the baby of the family. Connie was still more interested in Barbie dolls than boys.

The sisters occasionally had ferocious spats. Lorrie broke one of Connie's toes during one clash and Connie split Lorrie's lip with a broom during another. But their disagreements were over and forgotten as quickly as they flared. And Lorrie would react with pint-sized fury when other children made cruel fun of Connie's scoliosis.

The Sagers were equally quick to scrap with each other – and to rush to each other's aid. That very afternoon, an older neighbor had struck Debbie on the arm with a flail-like martial arts weapon called nunchukas. The resulting argument quickly drew Chris and Tommy in on their stepsister's side.

Although Debbie and Connie were the same age, Connie often was odd-man-out during Debbie's visit. Connie's mother attributed this to her more lethargic nature.

"Connie's favorite things were reading, television and food," Betty said. "If Debbie and Lorrie wanted to go on a long bike ride, Connie would stay home. If they were walking to the store for a Popsicle, Connie was along."

When Connie opened the car door in the pre-dawn dark, Debbie and Lorrie invited her to get in the back seat with them. Connie said no, she wanted to go inside.

Lorrie considered going inside too. The closed car windows made the vehicle's vinyl interior seem sticky, and the duplex's air conditioning especially inviting. But Lorrie didn't want to give up the adventure she and Debbie had pleaded for.

When Lorrie sat up as her sister was getting out, she noticed an unfamiliar dark car parked on the court. She felt a twinge of uneasiness that something didn't seem right but she couldn't pinpoint what.

All the lights appeared to be on inside the Smith duplex, despite the hour. Across the street, the downstairs light was on at the Davis house too. Lorrie knew Mrs. Davis had a new baby, which probably explained who was up at that house and why.

The two girls remaining in the car heard the screen door and the heavier front door slam behind Connie. Debbie told her cousin to lock the car door if she was scared. They rearranged themselves as much as space allowed and went back to sleep. Huddled under a blanket, Lorrie clutched a baseball bat.

At 7:30, Lorrie and Debbie had been awakened by Chris and Tommy Sager shouting through the window that their mother was dead. Lorrie shifted herself around to look at Debbie. She did not believe the boys. But the girls were now completely awake and impressed by the boys' unflinching persistence. They went in the house and looked through the doorway that led into the living room.

Connie was lying on the couch, her torso and blood-streaked face turned toward the back of the tufted brown plastic couch. Two couch cushions partially covered her body.

Above her head, saturated with blood, was the neatly folded blanket she had used as a pillow. Her feet, still wearing her blue sneakers and pom-pom trimmed socks were crossed at the ankles. Her T-shirt, printed with small flowers, was pulled up under her arms. A pair of bloodstained shorts was wadded up on the floor.

Lorrie began to scream. She felt herself turned around, her face pressed tightly against the chest of a man – whether a paramedic or a compassionate neighbor she would not remember later – and quickly directed out of the house. Among the confusion and horror of the next few minutes she would remember seeing her brother. She shrieked out to him, "Connie's dead! Connie's dead!"

Sobbing and shouting, Butch broke and ran behind the duplex, Lorrie later recalled. "It took five cops to stop him," she said. One of them threw Butch to the ground.

CHAPTER 3

SPRINGFIELD, N.Y.

Betty Sauer grew up in Springville, N.Y., a tucked-away town so small no street address was needed for a letter to reach its destination. Telephoning a neighbor didn't require dialing. The operator, more than likely an acquaintance, connected one five-digit number to another.

Small farms and a knife factory offered the only jobs available. A shopping trip meant an expedition to Sears Roebuck in Orchard Park. Strangers were a rarity and relatives abounded.

"If you look back far enough, everybody in Springville is related," Betty said.

Betty Sauer was the middle child of three. She had an older brother and a sister, Sharon, who was 16 months younger.

Sharon and her brother were tall, robust redheads. Tiny blond Betty, even on tiptoe, would never grow to reach five feet. Her brother dubbed her "Tinkerbell."

"I was the older sister, but I was the little sister," Betty said.

For the first few years of her life, the family lived on her grandfather's farm. Betty toddled after the old man as he went about his chores. She picked up a substantial German vocabulary in the process. Her kindergarten teacher advised Betty's father Carl, who also spoke fluent German, to speak only English until the child was well-grounded in that language too.

Her father, whom Betty described as "old-world strict," moved his wife and children to their own farm when Betty was five. He supported his family hauling gasoline to filling stations in Buffalo. At various times, he tried dairy farming and bee keeping. But eventually, the Sauers only farmed enough to provide for their own table. Among the children's chores was keeping the cellar filled with the wood used to heat their home.

Although Sauer was a stern disciplinarian who could terrify a misbehaving Betty with a glance, he rarely struck his children. But all three children were soundly spanked when their father caught them using his car's front fender for a sliding board. The studs on the children's jeans scratched the chrome.

"It was the only brand-new car father ever owned," Betty explained.

Betty loved her father but she adored her mother.

Beatrice Sauer had very clear ideas about what was appropriate conduct for girls. She tried to forbid Sharon and Betty from working in the barns with the cattle, but the girls frequently disobeyed.

"In our family, my brother loved to cook and we girls liked to work outside."

The Sauers never argued in front of their children. Betty realized later that they postponed their disagreements until the children were asleep behind closed, sound-baffling doors.

The children attended a Catholic grade school. Sharon and her brother did extremely well with minimal study. Betty struggled. She was held back one year, and because the school had only one class for that grade, was put in Sharon's class.

Sharon's impulsiveness, a quality she would not outgrow, made school even more difficult for Betty. Sharon would cajole her sister into skipping school with her.

"One day we skipped school and dyed each other's hair,"

Betty recalled. "We were just seeing what we could get away with, I guess."

Sharon's grades could accommodate such larks. Betty's could not.

Betty fell further and further behind.

"I just didn't catch on fast enough," she said.

The school enforced policies that were not uncommon then but would be considered abusive today. Betty said she still has scars on her knuckles from being rapped with a ruler. The blows were an effort to break her of a tendency to write with her left hand. She felt that because she was a poor student she was subjected to more frequent reprimands than the smart but mischievous Sharon.

Things reached a crisis when a nun Betty still recalls with a shudder caught Sharon and Betty talking in line, contrary to school rules. The woman, who Betty said had recently arrived from a teaching stint at a boys' correctional school, grabbed Betty and shoved her against the coat hooks bolted into the wall.

The next morning Betty's father came into her room armed with his belt after hearing that his daughter refused to get up and go to school. Her brother urged their father to look at Betty's back. Sauer was horrified at the bruises left by the coat hooks.

Betty said her parents confronted the school principal. Her non-Catholic mother did not conceal her fury when she was told "there must be some explanation." Betty said her father, reared to yield to clerical authority, was mortified by his wife's outburst. They withdrew Betty from the school, but allowed Sharon to remain.

Betty's grades improved in public school, which grouped the children according to their levels of skill.

When she was 13, Betty began working as a Candy Stripe girl in a Victorian-era house that had been converted into a nursing home. Her interest evolved naturally because her maternal grandmother had been a nurse and midwife.

Too, Candy Stripe girls received a small wage for their work during the summer, a happy incentive for a girl who'd found little reward in school work. And even more appealing, Betty had found something she was good at.

During high school, Sharon and Betty both attended the school dances, but Betty did not share her sister's enthusiasm for sporting events. They did share boyfriends occasionally, not an extraordinary situation in a small town.

One evening Betty had the uncomfortable task of telling a young man who'd arrived for a date with Sharon that the capricious girl had gone out with another. His name was James Smith and he took Betty out instead.

"He wasn't happy about it, but he got over it," Betty wryly added.

Betty thought that Smith was wonderfully sophisticated. He was from Orchard Park, a suburb of Buffalo, which, to Betty, seemed as worldly as coming from Paris or Hong Kong.

"He drove a red convertible and had all the right lines, things we weren't used to," Betty said with a laugh.

Jim and Betty ran off to Oregon together while Betty was a senior in high school. Jim had a cousin there and for a while it was great fun. But the couple lost what little possessions they had in a flood and were forced to return to Springville. "I knew we better be married when I came back," Betty said. And they were.

Their first child, Butch, was born two years later. Betty was delighted with her baby boy. She chose Sharon to be his godmother.

"He weighed seven pounds even, and was 21 inches long. For me that was a big baby. It seemed like he was always hungry."

While Betty tended her baby, Sharon mourned her young husband who had died in a hit-and-run accident shortly after Butch was born. The couple had run out of gas and were walking for help when a speeding car swerved toward them. Sharon's husband flung her toward a ditch, and safety, but was fatally injured himself.

"My sister never came out of it," Betty said. "Nothing worked for her after that."

A strange episode that happened when Butch was less than

a month old may have indicated that Sharon's grief had triggered a nervous breakdown.

"I'd left Butch with a babysitter," Betty said. "When I got back, they were both gone. I called the sitter and she said Sharon had come by. Sharon had told the sitter I'd said she could take the baby.

"I phoned Sharon but there was no answer. I went over to her house but no one answered the bell."

Betty was concerned but did not panic because she was confident Sharon would never harm her small godson. Finally, she guessed that Sharon must be in her apartment with the baby, not responding to the phone or the doorbell. She called the police who coaxed Sharon into relinquishing the child.

"She just needed something to love," Betty said of the strange episode.

Her sister's attachment to Butch remained strong, Betty said. Sharon would come and get him for weekend visits and never failed to remember his birthday. But her devotion later presented a problem after Betty had two other children who were not similarly favored by their aunt. Sharon shrugged off Betty's objections to the partiality. She felt Butch's status as godson rated special attention.

Betty gave birth to her first daughter, Lorrie, two years after Butch was born. Connie arrived 16 months after Lorrie.

Her husband, who wanted no more children, was surprised and not pleased when she became pregnant with Connie, Betty later recalled. Even she was surprised. She had been fitted with an inter-uterine birth control device.

The marriage had begun to deteriorate, Betty said, when her husband started working as a trucker. The job presented separations – and temptations – that the relationship could not survive. Betty had suspected all was not well, but was devastated when her husband left her after Connie was born.

"My whole life collapsed," she said.

Butch later said he remembered being bewildered when his mother told him that his father was leaving and not coming back. Only six at the time, he began to exhibit behavior that would later be interpreted as either a normal reaction to being abandoned or indicative of a disturbed mind, depending on the interpreter.

Not long after his father left, Butch set fire to the drapes in the trailer where he was living with his mother and sisters. Betty believed Butch was playing with a cigarette lighter and the fire began accidentally. Years later, others would see it differently.

Butch's sense of rejection by his father was profound. His behavior sometimes reflected his view that the world was a treacherous and disappointing place.

His father brought him presents on his seventh birthday, but then moved away. He did not see Butch again until the week before Connie's death years later.

Betty supported her family on food stamps, Medicaid and her meager salary as a nursing assistant. Her parents occasionally helped her, but Betty was determined to care for her children herself.

After the death of Sharon's first husband, Sharon had married Dennis Dash, who had been a classmate of her brother. Dash tended bar at a bowling alley. Sharon and Dennis had two children, Tyler and Debbie, before they broke up.

Betty was never sure why her sister's marriage eventually went sour. She thought, perhaps, that Sharon had married "on the rebound" before adjusting to the loss of her first husband.

Sharon's children and Betty's children played together frequently, and their grandparents liked nothing better than seeing the quintet scampering around their farm.

Having had difficulties in school herself, Betty was both anxious and sympathetic when Butch had problems adapting to the demands of classroom routine. As a result of his frequent temper tantrums, he was given a psychological evaluation in October, 1975, when he was nine years old. The tests revealed him to be of normal intelligence but exhibiting "aggressive tendencies, inconsistency and disturbed masculine strivings."

"He confabulated (lied) during the interview, making untrue, grandiose claims," the report said. This was the first official indication of a propensity for lying that would emerge again and again.

A happier aspect of Betty's life during that time was the renewed acquaintance with another former high school classmate. Coincidentally – or, perhaps, not so coincidentally, Betty later mused – he too was named James Smith. When Betty and he began dating, Smith, a Vietnam veteran, had just left the Marine Corps. Smith's experiences during the war had wrought profound changes in the small-town boy Betty had known in school. Not all of the changes were positive, Betty later would realize.

Butch met his prospective stepfather at the farm owned by Smith's parents. There, to his delight, he learned to shoot a bow and arrow.

After her second marriage, all went well at first for Betty, her children and new husband. They were living in Lancaster, N.Y. Smith was doing well working as a building subcontractor. But soon the jobs seemed to evaporate. Smith decided to re-enlist in the Marine Corps. It would prove to be a fateful decision.

The newly merged family moved to Camp Lejeune, N.C., in April 1976. Later, Betty would blame some of the couple's subsequent unhappiness on stresses related to the Marine Corps lifestyle. Smith was frequently gone for weeks or months at a time, she said. And he seemed more authoritarian each time he returned.

"We got along so well and then it was like the Marine Corps changed him," Betty recalled. "He ran his home like a drill instructor runs a platoon."

Another negative, Betty maintained, was the Marine Corps' subtle encouragement of "hard drinking."

"Every time you turned around, they were having a beer bash or something. It just got out of control."

Betty said her husband became abusive to her and the children when he drank. But she did not leave.

"I had no place to go. And I didn't want to admit I'd failed again.

Betty had consulted with base guidance counselors about Butch's previous poor performance and behavioral problems as soon as the Smiths moved to Lejeune. She had great hopes that Butch's school work would improve in his new environment. But it was not to be so.

Butch was first suspended, for disrespect to a teacher, in the fall of 1976. He was 10.

Like his mother, Butch was terrified and confused by the change alcohol engendered in his stepfather.

In September 1977, when Butch was 11, Betty took him to the Lejeune naval hospital with bruises on his buttocks. According to the medical report, Butch said his dad had made him do "Marine push-ups," striking him with a paddle as he performed the exercise. When questioned, Smith admitted hitting the boy for "mouthing off." The family was referred to the hospital's child advocacy committee and Butch began to see a school counselor regularly.

In a written report, the counselor alluded to the hostility in the Smith home and Smith's alcoholism. Butch "was anxious about the fact that his stepfather would strike his mother after drinking and verbally abuse her and others in the family," the counselor reported.

The fear and resentment Butch felt for his stepfather was mingled with an idealized love for Smith, whom he always referred to as "Dad." Butch was never so happy as when his stepfather would take him on fishing trips and to ball games. Smith taught Butch the basics of auto mechanics and occasionally the pair hunted for small game in the vast forests at Camp Lejeune. And Butch was enraptured by the Vietnam war stories Smith recounted.

But Butch later would tell a psychiatrist that he was terrified when his dad experienced what Butch described as "flashbacks" to Vietnam. Butch said he once saw his dad climb up on a bed and aim a rifle at an unseen enemy. At other times, Butch said, Smith would crawl through the house, as if looking for Viet Cong.

The boy felt confused and helpless when Smith challenged him to competitions in wrestling or bow marksmanship or "mock" hand-to-hand combat. Butch said Smith intended to make "one tough Marine" out of him. But the tall, lanky boy was hardly a match for a well-muscled staff sergeant.

"I want to become a Force Recon like my dad," Butch later would say. "In some ways you have to be good; in some ways you have to be bad."

Betty's worries webbed out beyond her marital relationship. Butch's problems at school were increasingly serious. He was repeatedly suspended.

Betty recognized that her chaotic marriage was contributing to Butch's problems. But she also attributed at least some of Butch's difficulties to an atmosphere that she felt glorified male aggression. "You've got to remember, he comes from a very violent walk of life" she said. "I mean Marine Corps life is not exactly what I call a calm, passive way to raise children."

Grace Crichton* was one of Butch's sixth-grade teachers. "A teacher will have several children who stand out in her mind" she later recalled. "He's definitely one who stands out in my mind. I knew he was a problem from the beginning because of his records. His mother was very cooperative. She wanted to help but seemed unable to control him.

"He could be sweet and kind and then mean and hateful. He'd be good, sit there and behave, and then do something off the wall, laugh hysterically and then go back to work as though nothing had happened.

"He was Dr. Jekyll and Mr. Hyde. He might throw a spitball or a book or chair at someone, pull someone's chair out from under them and laugh when they fell on the floor.

"He was in the low-average class academically. But I looked at my old grade book not too long ago and I saw he could do the work when he wanted to.

"I've seen him chase children across the playground and knock them down. Once, he tried to turn a bookcase over on a child after the child said something that upset him. But he didn't hold a grudge. A minute later it would all be forgotten.

"Some of the kids were afraid of him because of his size, but he wasn't isolated. The kids would play with him at recess.

"I must say, I never felt threatened by him. And he never really talked ugly to me. When I disciplined him, he would mind me. But it just wouldn't last."

In March of 1978, when he was 12, Butch was evaluated by a Navy psychiatrist, who met with him twice monthly for several months. According to the doctor's evaluation, "Butch revealed a very poor self-image and a tendency to become very aggressive as a compensatory defense against his sensitivity and inadequacy."

Butch's difficulty in controlling his aggressive tendencies was noted, as was "a persistent mistrust of people, particularly male authority figures."

Physical examinations revealed a possible "epileptic equivalent" which, according to the psychiatrist, might result in behavioral difficulties.

Dilantin, often used to treat hyperactivity in children, was prescribed for Butch. But the drug only brought about a worsening of symptoms. Trial use of other drugs yielded no improvement.

Psychiatric treatment ended in a stalemate, with Butch diagnosed as "Borderline Character Disorder."

There was another treatment alternative. Base school officials, with Betty's cooperation, applied to the N.C. Department of Human Resources Therapeutic Wilderness Camp System on Butch's behalf in April, 1979. As a result, Butch was sent to the Eckerd Wilderness Camp in Newport, N.C., a residential program for emotionally disturbed boys, ages 10-17.

It was later rumored that Butch was sent to the camp because he struck a teacher, a rumor Butch may have encouraged because the teacher was not popular with students. Grace Crichton, however, said it was an accumulation of behavioral problems, not a specific incident that prompted the decision.

Butch had mixed feelings about being sent to the camp. He was relieved to be free of the demands of school. But he felt he was being abandoned by his family because he had failed to meet their expectations.

The Eckerd Camp features intensive group therapy in an outdoors environment. Although not as harsh as "survivalist" programs, boys must build their own shelters and cook by campfire.

The philosophy is to direct the boys away from destructive

behavior toward more socially acceptable ways of dealing with conflict.

The boys, in groups of 10, concentrate their energies on activities such as rafting, canoeing and backpacking. Contact sports are not permitted. Drugs are forbidden at the camp, as is smoking.

"You couldn't even chew gum," Butch said.

Butch later was depicted as an avid reader of *Soldier of Fortune* magazine. Some later would say his interest indicated a proclivity for violence. But, at least during the 18 months he spent at the camp, he had little opportunity to read the magazine. The one issue he tried to take into the camp was confiscated.

"The only magazines we could read were *Boys' Life* and *Hot Rod*," Butch said.

Butch told a counselor that he had the book *Helter Skelter* at home and was familiar with the Manson killings. The book was, indeed, found on a dining room bookshelf in the Smith quarters after the murders and the book's presence would be viewed as ominous by some investigators. But his mother later said she had been loaned the book by a co-worker at the nursing home who warned that she probably wouldn't get through 20 pages because it was "heavy reading."

"She was right," Betty said. "I don't think I got through 10 pages."

Every six weeks, the boys at the Eckerd camp were allowed to go home from Friday until Tuesday. If they had seriously misbehaved, the privilege could be revoked. According to a counselor's report, Butch looked forward to going home, but in the months before his stepfather was reassigned to Okinawa, he was sometimes anxious about what kind of reception he would get from his dad.

By the same token, some of the happiest home visits during that time included outings with his dad, Butch later recalled. But most of his visits were, at best, stressful. A photograph taken the Christmas after Butch entered the camp shows Betty and her children posed before a handsomely decorated tree. Betty, wan and pretty, has her hands folded in front of her and only a faint suggestion of a smile. Beside her, Connie glances up from beneath thick blond bangs, shyly smiling. Behind them are a somber Lorrie and a decidedly glum Butch.

Butch ran away from camp twice. Each time, he returned home, believing he could convince his mother that his behavior had changed enough that he need not return to camp. He was crushed when Betty notified camp directors and made him go back. After the second time he ran away, Butch was punished by not being allowed his next scheduled home visit.

Fights at the camp were daily occurrences and Butch, according to his exaggerated reckoning, was in 100 fights in a year and a half. An official report says the incidence was about once a month.

"You put 10 people together with the same problems, you get fights," Butch explained.

According to camp policy, the acceptable alternative to fighting was talking. Group discussions and individual counseling were sometimes as exhausting and painful as a slug fest.

"We'd talk about a problem until you just couldn't talk anymore," Butch said.

During the latter half of their stay, when the boys catch up on the academic studies that are secondary to behavior modification earlier in the program, they enjoyed a bit more freedom. Later, Butch would happily remember a field trip to Kitty Hawk, N.C., and the attendant privilege of wearing sneakers instead of camp boots.

There are obvious limitations to juvenile rehabilitation programs such as the wilderness camp. The child's problems may be too deep-seated for any limited-term treatment. And the child is returned to the same situation from which his problems emerged. Both limitations affected Butch's case.

A psychiatric evaluation done before he left the camp was not encouraging. Butch, it said, had benefited "but retained a considerable amount of anger and resentment, particularly relating to feelings about his family." Butch was described in the report as "a tall young man who interacted in a cooperative fashion, although his attitude was that of chip-on-his-shoulder, 'wise guy' character."

The psychiatrist described the prognosis as guarded and recommended that therapy continue when Butch left the camp. The diagnosis was "adjustment reaction of adolescence."

Betty was relieved when her husband was sent to Okinawa for a tour of duty that did not include his family. She waited until he was overseas to tell him the marriage was over. She and the children were allowed to remain in quarters until her problems with her husband could be resolved.

Meanwhile, Betty worked at a Jacksonville nursing home, frequently on a night shift.

"The kids would come into my bedroom in the morning and watch cartoons and eat a bowl of cereal while I slept," Betty recalled. "They were used to me working nights. At noon, they knew mom would wake up and off to the beach we'd go."

Betty thought it unlikely that a reconciliation with her husband was possible. But when this marriage was over, she intended to be better prepared to provide for her family. Soon after she filed for separation, she started classes at the community college in Jacksonville, hoping to become a registered nurse.

She worked part-time as a bartender in addition to her job at the nursing home. The tips were wonderful, she said, and her work hours flexible.

The bar where she worked was no lure to sleek couples seeking a romantic nightspot. But it was not as rough and tumble as many of the bars that spring up near military installations.

Although it later would become a topless drinkery, its front windows painted over, in 1981 it still catered to retirees and non-commissioned officers who liked to down a few beers while rehashing adventures in Korea and Vietnam. It was reputed to serve the best hamburger in town.

It was while tending bar that Betty met Gary Francis, who, like Smith, was a Marine staff sergeant.

"You know, all these guys come in with sad stories," Betty

recalled. "And Gary had such a sad story. He seemed very nice, good-looking, had three kids and was separated from his wife. He knew all the right things to say. And, I guess, was there when I needed him."

The relationship intensified quickly. Gary shared a mobile home with another Marine. Betty and Gary would frequently meet there. It was some time before Betty brought Gary home, but Betty's daughters were soon included in their activities such as beach outings and trips to the store for ice cream.

Butch met Francis during a home visit from the camp. Much to the boy's delight, Francis took him to the drag races. At first, Butch assumed Francis was just one of his mother's friends. But he soon suspected the relationship was more than casual and confronted her about it.

"Are you seeing someone besides my dad?" he asked.

Betty answered, "Yes, I am."

"I got used to him after a while," Butch later said of Francis. "I started to like him for a while too. But he still wasn't my dad."

During a home visit over the Christmas holidays, Butch made a friend whose loyalty would never fail. Tom Cheek had known Lorrie since the two shared a math class in junior high. Tom could see the back doors of the Smith residence from his own home, and he occasionally stopped by to see Lorrie, who he thought was very nice. He thought Connie a little spoiled. "If she didn't get her way, she'd get mad."

Of Betty, Tom would recall: "She was real nice but if you messed up, she'd let you know it."

Lorrie's brother Butch, Tom heard, was in "reform school," but when the two met, they hit it off immediately. Tom, who was small for his age, enjoyed being with the much taller Butch. When Butch visited Tom's house for the first time, Tom's Mother, Mary Cheek, quipped, "Where'd you find this giant, Tom?"

Mary recalled Butch as being unfailingly polite to her. She saw no unusual behavior when the Smith children and her children played hide-and-seek in her yard, as they frequently did.

"He was a lot of fun," said Tom. "We'd explore the trails

through the woods, things boys do. Once, we put a boat model in the water and threw rocks at it, like torpedoes, to see if we could sink it.

"One time he threw a shotgun shell on a little fire, after showing everybody what he was going to do, and everybody scattered. One time, we went around late at night ringing doorbells to wake people up and then ran away."

Tom insisted he and Butch never stole or vandalized anything. And, if Butch was using marijuana, he kept it from him, Tom said.

"We did the kinds of things that would have gotten us a good chewing out, not arrested," Tom recalled.

The boys were soon spending the weekends at each other's homes. And after the Sagers arrived, Tom also would befriend Tyler.

Mary Cheek was never afraid to have Butch in her house although some of her neighbors were horrified when she continued to allow his visits after the killings. Mary had two daughters younger than Tom.

In mid-July of 1981, Betty got a call at the nursing home where she worked. It was Connie. Betty was mildly annoyed because she had told the children not to call her at work unless it was urgent. She expected Connie had called to complain about some squabble with Lorrie.

"But, Mommy, I've got a surprise. Aunt Sharon's here." Betty was flabbergasted.

She knew Sharon's third husband, Fred Sager, was in Alaska with the U.S. Army. He supposedly was making arrangements for Sharon and the children to join him there.

Sharon's children now numbered six. They included: Tyler and Debbie Dash; Fred Sager's two sons from a former marriage; and the two pre-schoolers he and Sharon had together.

Betty had not yet confided in Sharon that she intended to divorce Smith. But from their phone calls, Betty had deduced that Sharon's marriage was floundering too.

There were now eight children in the Smith duplex. And

Butch was due to be released from the Eckerd camp in three weeks.

Betty's suspicions about Sharon's marriage were confirmed by the tenor of the phone calls between Sharon and Fred Sager. Sharon would pull the kitchen telephone into the laundry room and shut the door, but the angry nature of the calls was unmistakable.

Betty encouraged a young Marine she'd befriended to act as an informal escort for Sharon when she and Betty and Francis went out together. The corporal, who said he considered Betty a "mother figure," had a platonic relationship with both women. He occasionally saw Sharon in the company of other men but thought little of it.

On Monday, August 10, Betty, Sharon and their eight children drove to the Eckerd camp to get Butch.

It was not until his aunt's station wagon, filled to overflowing with sisters and cousins, arrived to take him home that Butch knew the Sagers were staying with his mother.

If Butch had anticipated enjoying a greater privacy and independence when he returned home, he was disappointed. Of Butch's reunion with Connie, Betty later recalled: "It was fine. No different than before." And Lorrie? "They started off great. Fighting and arguing like always."

But Butch was shaken by the confusing onslaught of relatives. He particularly resented the communal takeover of his possessions.

"I know Butch was upset over the kids tearing his room up," Betty said. And Butch had a battle royal with Tyler when Tyler rode Butch's cherished 10-speed over a curb and bent the wheel.

Tom Cheek, Butch's best friend, witnessed the fracas over Butch's bike. He said it was not serious.

"It's like if your little sister takes your toy and plays with it after you tell her not to. You get mad at her – but you don't kill her."

Even more aggravating, the Sager youngsters, while rough-housing, had damaged a ship model that Butch and his dad had begun together and Butch had finished.

But Butch was not the only member of the family disturbed by the chaotic combination of cousins in the small duplex.

"Lorrie got into a screaming match with my sister over the kids," Betty said. Sharon's two small sons had applied red paint to Betty's car and the front of the duplex. "Sharon told the older girls to clean it off, which they felt was unfair."

But of all the children, Tyler may have been the most unhappy with the living arrangements. An intelligent, good-looking but overweight youth, Tyler until recently had been living with his father. His mother was very displeased with the weight her son had gained and his complexion problems that she attributed to poor eating habits. She chided the boy for being like his father, who was also obese. "The more she yelled, the more he became withdrawn," Betty said.

Betty said Tyler's attitude contributed to his unhappiness. "Tyler wasn't trying to fit in. He would lie on the couch in the playroom and didn't want to do anything," she recalled. There is no indication that Connie was fonder of Tyler than any of the other boy cousins. But it would not have been surprising if Tyler and Connie, both overweight, were sympathetic to each other. They both endured insensitive remarks from the other children and, in Tyler's case, criticism from his mother.

Connie was a friendly child who craved the approving attention of family and friends.

"My youngest one was a very physically affectionate person," Betty said of Connie. "She liked to be held and rocked. You know, she wouldn't think nothing of crawling up in your lap and cuddling up and going to sleep. It's just the way Connie was. She was a very affectionate child. Connie trusted everybody."

Much to Betty's chagrin, the military police were summoned more than once because of the noise created by the Smiths and their numerous house guests. Butch later said one of his first objectives on arriving home from the camp had been to escape the crowd and find Bennie,* his source of marijuana.

31

According to Butch, he began smoking marijuana during a weekend leave from the Eckerd camp. Bennie had walked up to the younger boy and asked, "Have you ever tried this stuff?" Butch's first smoke was unremarkable. "I thought, big deal," he recalled. But Bennie coaxed him into trying it again several days later and this time Butch's reaction was "Wow." Bennie told Butch, "If you ever want any more, I'll get it for you."

Bennie's intent, of course, was to recruit a new customer. And he succeeded. "Marijuana was my way of escaping," Butch later said. "I felt good when I was high, but coming down I was irritable and lippy."

Butch had been home less than 24 hours when Sharon again shaped the family's plans. Betty received a message through a co-worker at the nursing home that Betty's father had suffered a heart attack and Betty must come to New York immediately.

Betty anxiously rushed home to discover an amused Sharon packing the station wagon. When Betty began to tell her sister about their father's heart attack, Sharon laughed and said it had been a joke. "She said I needed a vacation and it was the only way she could think of to get me home from work," Betty said.

Betty was relieved, of course, that her father was not really ill. But she was astounded that her sister could have manipulated her in such a cruel way. She angrily told her sister what she thought of her maneuvers. But her anger passed. And the persuasive Sharon soon convinced Betty it would be great fun for them and the children to visit the grandparents in New York.

The two women and nine children drove to New York on August 11. While they were there, a stream of family and friends dropped by to see them and the children. The Sauer home was even more crowded than the duplex at Camp Lejeune. But the Sauers reveled in having so much of the family together.

Butch corded wood for his grandparents. He later said he considered himself well-paid for his labors.

The girls slept in the room with Betty. "The babies" – Sharon's two pre-schoolers – slept with their mother except for the two days when, without explanation, Sharon disappeared. Her parents were terribly worried, Betty said, but when Sharon returned, she would not discuss where she had been.

Debbie and Tyler had dinner with their father, Dennis Dash, shortly before the children left New York to return to North Carolina. Lorrie, Connie and Butch also saw their natural father, whom they had not seen in eight years, and the girls seemed more curious than excited about it. They scarcely remembered him. But Butch desperately wanted his father's approval, Betty said. Disillusioned with the stepfather he nonetheless idolized, Butch hoped his real father would offer the acceptance for which he yearned. Butch grew noticeably dispirited when his father was late arriving. When he finally arrived, Butch introduced himself by saying, "Remember me? I'm your son."

Butch later said he was crushed when his father replied, "Funny, you'd never know it to look at you."

When Smith implied that it was Betty's moving away that had limited his contact with the three children, Betty did not argue. "I only wanted peace," she said.

Butch and Connie went with their father to the state fair. Lorrie had become ill and was unable to go. The fair was exciting and their father congenial but Butch grew uneasy when he seemed reluctant to let Connie and him return to their mother. Connie later told Betty that she cried when her father told her he wanted them to stay with him. Butch, too, was relieved to get back to his grandparents'.

The family returned to Camp Lejeune on August 22. Some friends of Sharon later said she'd told them she didn't intend to go back. A photograph taken the day before the Sagers and Smiths returned from New York shows a group of smiling, handsome blond children. The two youngest Sagers have identical mops of flaxen hair. Long-limbed Lorrie sits beside the four Sager boys on the floor. On the couch behind them, a beaming Connie is wedged between Debbie and a New York cousin. Butch is leaning back, grinning, one arm draped around Tyler's shoulder. Tyler's head is resting casually against Butch's arm.

During the drive to Lejeune, Betty later recalled, her sister said something that made her uneasy.

"Take the kids and get the hell out of that house," Sharon told her. Despite her pleas, Betty could not get her sister to explain what she meant. She presumed Sharon was worried about how Betty's husband would react when he learned of her relationship with Gary Francis.

For Butch and the other children, the return trip in the station wagon, crammed with 11 people in August heat, was predictably miserable. Thirty minutes from Lejeune, the children's restless excitement reached an unusually noisy pitch.

"If you don't get quiet, we can take three hours to get home," Sharon teased.

The trailer park where Gary Francis lived was a mile from the base main gate and about three miles from the housing area where the Smiths lived. Sharon dropped Betty off there before continuing to the Kentucky Court duplex. Later, Betty and Francis also returned to the duplex, and Sharon went back to the trailer with them. Sharon stayed to watch television with a few of Francis' friends until about 4:00 p.m. when she returned to Kentucky Court. At 6:00, Francis took Betty to the nursing home where she was scheduled to work an overnight shift.

Butch's friend Tom Cheek was delighted that his big buddy was home. His own family was planning to leave on a fishing trip Sunday, so Tom spent that Saturday night at Butch's house.

"We stayed up late, watched a movie, ate popcorn," Tom later recalled.

He remembered that Debbie, Lorrie and Connie wanted to spend the night in the station wagon, but changed their minds after an unfamiliar car raced around the court on squealing tires. That night, Tom slept on the playroom couch where Sharon Sager would be murdered one day later.

Sunday, after Tom went home, Sharon took her older boys and Butch on a shopping expedition and bought each a pellet gun. That afternoon Butch and Tyler got into a squabble that would remain a matter of dispute for years. Butch later would claim he came into the house as Sharon was angrily herding

Tyler and Connie downstairs from the direction of the upstairs bathroom. He got the impression Sharon had caught the two children "playing doctor or post office."

According to Butch, Sharon sent Tyler and Connie into separate rooms for an hour. Butch said his aunt also spoke to Connie behind the closed laundry room door. He did not overhear the conversation but Connie was crying when she emerged a few minutes later.

Butch said he waited in the front yard until Tyler came outside. "You like screwing other people's sisters?" Butch recalled shouting at his cousin. "You screw your own sister and leave my sister alone."

Tyler "lipped off" at him, Butch said, and the argument escalated. A wrestling match ensued. According to Butch, the fight was witnessed by several neighbors. A friend's father broke it up, Butch said. Although Butch was taller, he and Tyler weighed the same and neither boy was injured. Butch said Sharon later made the boys apologize to each other.

Neighbors and Butch's friend Tom Cheek did later remember the boys fighting, either Saturday or Sunday morning. But no one, including the man Butch claimed broke up the fight, recalled a shouting match about Connie.

After being reprimanded by his mother, Tyler angrily demanded that Sharon let him call his father. He was permitted to do so. During that phone call, according to Tyler's father, Dennis Dash, Tyler said he had caught Butch "in bed" with Connie.

During the time when Tyler was being punished and making the phone call to his father, Butch and Bennie went down the street into a wooded area where the two boys smoked marijuana.

Francis picked Betty up from work Sunday afternoon and drove her to the duplex to shower and change before the couple went out to dinner. Sharon told them to enjoy themselves because it was the last time she'd baby sit. She did not mention the incident with Connie and Tyler.

Butch did complain to his mother that he was sick of a house full of relatives, and Betty reprimanded him for being rude. Later that night, when Betty called home from a convenience store near Gary's trailer, she could hear the children making a racket in the background.

"I've got to quiet these kids down before the neighbors complain," Sharon told Betty.

Betty said her sister was very calm, more self-possessed than she'd been during the entire visit.

"She told me that she planned to leave the next morning and return to Kansas. She said she'd talked to a friend who told her she could get her old job back."

Betty also spoke to Lorrie and Connie. They told their mother of their plans to sleep in the car with Debbie.

Betty had intended to return to Kentucky Court that night but changed her mind.

During Sharon's visit, Betty usually slept on the couch in the playroom and let Sharon sleep in the master bedroom. Which lights were left on during the night depended on who was last to bed, Betty said. Lorrie would leave just the kitchen stove light burning. Only the faintest of illumination would spill over the kitchen counter into the playroom.

"If Connie was the last one to go to sleep, the house could look like a Christmas tree," Betty said.

While the Sagers were visiting, the downstairs bathroom light was left on so the two smallest children wouldn't bump into anything if they needed to use the toilet.

Betty also generally left on the light in the upstairs bathroom.

Butch later said that he went outside to smoke dope at 12:30 a.m. "to help me go to sleep."

When he returned, the girls in the station wagon called to him and asked him to bring them glasses of water. He brought them a canteen instead.

When he went back in the house, he said, Tyler and Chris were still downstairs. Butch went upstairs to his room, where Tommy was listening to the radio in the top bunk.

On the morning of August 24, Francis planned to let Betty off at the duplex, report to his unit for 8:00 a.m. physical training, then pick Betty up afterwards and take her to a doctor's appointment. When they arrived at the blocked-off cul-de-sac and saw the ambulance pulled up to the Smiths' door, Betty leaped from the car and ran toward the house. She was stopped by a military policeman before she reached it.

According to Francis, an NIS agent approached him and said, "I'm going to be quite frank with you, Sgt. Francis. Three people were cut to ribbons in that house last night."

Betty would later remember sitting in a car, stricken and weeping, with a Navy chaplain. She looked up and saw Butch standing alone at the corner of the house. The other children had been taken to the naval hospital.

When Betty got to the hospital, she was allowed to use an open phone line to call family members, including Dennis Dash, to tell them what had happened. "It was probably the hardest thing I ever had to do," Betty said.

Not until that night was she interviewed by NIS agents. By then she was too exhausted to note that more of their questions concerned Butch than the other children.

When the seven surviving children were released to her custody that night, Betty took them to Gary's trailer at his invitation. They would spend two nights in the trailer before being placed in protective custody at the Hostess House on base. "The children had no toothbrushes, no clothes except what they were wearing," Betty recalled. The older children, she said, were very keyed up, asking endless questions and exchanging bits of information they had garnered during the day. But they refused to sleep unless someone promised to stay awake.

"I'd wake up and they'd be curled up next to me, or lying at the foot of the bed," Betty said.

Sharon's two pre-schoolers seemed more bewildered than upset. "They kept asking, where's Mommy?" Betty said.

CHAPTER 4

THE INVESTIGATION

Because of the typically sluggish morning traffic, NIS Special Agent Mike Duncan* scarcely needed to brake when he reached the Camp Lejeune main gate. The MP sentry glimpsed the warrant officer's sticker on Duncan's car and snapped off the salute that allowed him to pass.

Dense clouds took the edge off the early-morning sunlight that usually pierced Duncan's windshield and forced him to flip down his visor. He drove with his car radio and a portable police radio on. He was adept at sorting out the trivial from the significant on the police radio, even with Waylon Jennings and a rattling air conditioner added to the mix.

The agent's ears prickled faintly when he caught the words "one body" and soon after, "got another body." His first thought was an automobile smash-up. Unfortunately, expressions of esprit de corps among young Marines often involved alcohol. And the long, four-lane stretch of Highway 24 leading to the base had tempted more than one well-lubricated Marine to speed.

When the cryptic radio message was repeated, the dispatcher's voice had a tight urgency that contrasted sharply with the usual Monday morning monotone. The additional words "at Watkins Village" spurred Duncan's interest considerably.

The agent maneuvered into the far-right lane and turned onto Brewster. He was less than five minutes from Watkins Village. By the time he pulled into the non-commissioned officers' housing area, the dispatcher had cited the specific address, 6080-A Kentucky Court.

MPs in precisely pressed uniforms, the khaki fabric punctuated by gold police badges, were already in front of the duplex door. The shrill whoop of an ambulance could be heard approaching from Hospital Point. When Duncan spotted NIS's sole female agent retching into the gutter in front of the apartment, he knew something horrific had happened.

A somber MP told Duncan there were three, not two bodies in the house. Several children, apparently, had notified a neighbor after discovering the bodies. The agent stepped into the duplex, warm sunlight spilling into the dim hallway ahead, to asses the gruesome scene for himself.

In a matter of days, Duncan, a former big-city cop, would become as coolly familiar with that scene as anyone involved in the case, but he would remember being staggered by the carnage during his first tour of the apartment.

"At a crime scene, I try to imagine myself as perpetrator of that crime," Duncan said. "But there was no way I could imagine myself as perpetrator of this crime."

He walked down the hallway into the den where a woman's body lay. Her nightgown clung to her skin through the adhesion of her own blood. The saturation had discolored the garment's original pastel blue to a grisly magenta.

It appeared the woman had green or hazel eyes and auburn hair. Beyond that, it was difficult to guess what she had looked like in life. A gaping wound disfigured the left side of her throat.

A beige brassiere with no apparent bloodstains was draped

casually over a footstool beside the couch. Duncan guessed the woman had removed the undergarment before lying down.

Her eyeglasses, finely spattered with blood, rested above her head. She wore a wedding band and a wristwatch. A few glancing cuts on her hand indicated she had tried to defend herself. But whoever killed her had moved so deliberately and quickly that the woman had scarcely disarranged the makeshift bedding. And the lamp adjacent to the couch had not been overturned despite the obvious fury of the assault.

Duncan's glance swept over the room. Droplets of blood were apparent on the light fixture suspended over the couch. A television, sitting on the built-in counter that separated the kitchen from the den, was turned off. The long cushions and one smaller cushion from the couch had been arranged to make a pallet on the floor across the room from where the woman lay. A fourth cushion and blanket were in the middle of the rug that covered most of the floor.

Duncan noted one of the investigative obstacles agents would face. The room and adjacent kitchen were cluttered. Clothes and toys were strewn on the floor where children had dropped them. The sink and kitchen counter were layered with dirty dishes and food-preparation debris. Among such disarray, it would be nearly impossible to determine what was missing or out of place.

Duncan walked out of the den and through the doorway to his left. He entered the dining room and walked toward the back of a couch that divided the dining room from the living room. The MP had indicated another female victim was in the living room. As Duncan came around the end of the couch, he saw a pair of small legs, crossed at the ankle, extended from beneath a couch cushion. The arrangement gave the curious impression that the body, which was that of a child, was pinned under the cushion, oppressed by its weight. A second cushion overlapped the first.

The coffee table directly in front of the couch had not been disturbed. The liquid contents of a glass resting on that table had not been spilled, causing Duncan to presume the girl had been attacked from over the back of the couch.

A spattering of blood trailed across the ceiling toward the dining room, perpendicular to the couch. This probably had resulted from the killer's slinging the knife back over his head during the assault, Duncan thought.

The girl's neck wounds were similar to the woman's, perhaps not as deep. Her left ear had been repeatedly slashed. Her eyes were closed, the long lashes flecked with blood. One hand was curled up like an infant's beside the wound in her neck.

Using a ballpoint pen, Duncan carefully lifted the cushion enough to allow him to see under it. His stomach roiled. The T-shirt she was wearing was pulled up beneath her arms. She was wearing no other clothing but a pair of athletic shoes and short socks with pom poms at the heels. The girl had apparently received the most terrible of her wounds after death, Duncan thought. A small mercy, in this house of horror. A gash deep enough to expose her intestines had been gouged from her genitals to her chest. Duncan assumed the wound was postmortem because little blood had flowed from it. But blood was smeared on her upper legs and between her thighs.

This type of wound, Duncan recognized, was the work of a sexual killer, the result of a specialized depravity that derived erotic pleasure from such vicious acts.

A pair of bloodstained shorts lay on the floor at the foot of the couch, Duncan noticed. And a woman's wallet was tossed on a small table near a window. Later Duncan would learn that the wallet, which contained $424, belonged to the dead woman.

Duncan turned aside. He could not imagine the third body being more distressing than this one.

An open stairwell was visible from the living room where the girl lay. Duncan walked up the short, straight flight of stairs. A small upstairs landing led to four bedrooms, a windowless bathroom and an oversized storage closet. The upstairs was as messy as the downstairs, Duncan noted. A few bloodstains were visible on towels and items of clothing lying on the floor of the landing.

The room where the third victim's body lay was to the left of the landing. The bed was adjacent to a large closet, so close,

Duncan noted, that it would have been a bit difficult to get in the closet. The headboard was set against a deep-set window ledge. Because of the feminine toys and clothing that dominated the room, Duncan assumed a girl usually slept there.

But it was a boy's body that lay on the bed. He had suffered throat wounds similar to the other victims. Like the woman, he appeared to have put up a fight. But, like the woman, the boy had been killed so quickly that his blanket was still in place.

Duncan's revulsion at the little girl's death had been mitigated somewhat by the realization that she had probably died in her sleep, unmindful of the danger. The boy, unfortunately, had known he was being attacked. But not for long.

Duncan was suddenly weary. The adrenalin that had braced him through the succession of harrowing sights was depleted. He realized his shirt collar, damp with sweat, had grown clammy in the air conditioned duplex. It was an uncomfortable feeling. He was relieved to get back outside to await instruction from his superiors.

Arnold Sleeper was the NIS Special Agent in Charge at Camp Lejeune. A former San Diego policeman, he was described by his admirers as articulate, demanding and extremely professional. His detractors thought him egotistical and overbearing. One officer with whom Sleeper worked described him as "The J.Edgar Hoover of Camp Lejeune." "The atmosphere at NIS changed after Sleeper's arrival," the officer said. "The agency was much less open. People became more close-mouthed."

A former company grade officer recalled: "When Sleeper first came on board, I spent a lot of time trying to figure out what I'd done to annoy him. After a while I realized that's just the way he was."

Sleeper was fastidious in his personal appearance, invariably wearing a white shirt with a collar pin.

"He was the quintessential man-in-the-gray-flannel-suit," said a former associate. "No matter how late he'd been out the night before, he was always on time and immaculately dressed. But he wasn't a personable guy."

Mike Jones, Sleeper's second-in-command, also was "a company man," but much better liked by his peers. Jones was the pat-on-the-back, Sleeper the bludgeon.

When Sleeper heard about the murders, on the morning of August 24, he hurriedly called in agents from their several sections – narcotics, crimes against property, crimes of violence, white collar crime – and assigned them to the case. Some 30 agents immediately fanned out to collect evidence, interview witnesses and track down leads.

A command post tent was erected in the center of Kentucky Court as a collection point for statements and evidence. Because of the heat, an improvised refreshment stand was set up for investigators under the canopy.

Hector Amos* was one of those investigators. He had just graduated from the Federal Law Enforcement Training Command in Glynco, Ga., in the spring of 1981, and was assigned to Camp Lejeune's Criminal Investigative Division. CID is the investigative branch of the military police which usually is responsible for investigating less serious on-base offenses, such as minor barracks thefts and simple assults. NIS assumes investigations of more serious crimes on Navy and Marine bases. NIS agents are civil servants. CID investigators are active-duty Marines who may temporarily be attached to the NIS as Amos was.

When he had arrived at NIS headquarters August 24, Amos had poured himself the morning's second jolt of coffee, noting that the office was nearly empty. He asked the only other special agent present what was going on.

"I think we have three bodies out in town."

"What do you mean, 'think?' " Amos said. "You do or you don't."

"Well, just stand by," the agent answered.

Both agents were soon summoned, not out in town but to Watkins Village.

"I figured I'd be a go-fer or something, but Jones told me to take one of the crime scenes," Amos recalled.

He requested that another CID agent, Bill Blakeney*, help him. The two men were responsible for the den/playroom where Sharon Sager's body was found.

"I happened to have a compass on," Amos said. "At CID school, the room where we practiced triangulation was set up with magnetic north set directly in front of you.

"When I walked in the room where the body was, north was directly in front of me. I said, OK, Bill, we're going to do this exactly like in school.' "

The agents took "360s," photographs of the entire room, and began rough sketches of the crime scene, showing the exact placement of evidence in relation to the walls. While they were doing that, the Navy doctor acting as medical examiner arrived and pronounced Sharon Sager dead at 8:34 a.m. Her body temperature was 97.8 degrees Fahrenheit.

After examining the other victims, the doctor, assisted by the staff pathologist and a hospital corpsman, began preparations to remove the woman's body.

Amos objected. "No way. We're not nearly finished processing the scene." An argument ensued and grew more heated until Sleeper came in and asked what the problem was.

The exasperated Amos explained. Sleeper turned to the medical examiner and said it would be necessary for the doctor to follow the agent's directions.

"That's the way it's going to be," Sleeper said.

While the threat of precipitous removal of the bodies had been deflected, the crime scene had already been undermined and worse "contamination" was to come.

Contamination describes accidental alterations of a crime scene. These alterations may obscure or destroy evidence. They also may create distracting false evidence, such as fingerprints left by a curious passer-by.

By the time the first NIS agents began their investigation at the apartment, many people had already broached the crime scene: the children who had alerted the neighbors; an indeterminate number of neighbors; and the MPs initially dispatched to the duplex. Of those, only the MPs were even remotely aware how crucial it is that a crime scene not be disturbed.

Another inadvertent contaminating factor arrived in the persons of the ambulance crew.

"The biggest enemy to protecting the crime scene 99 percent of the time is the ambulance crew," Mike Duncan later said.

According to rules governing emergency scenes in many places, civilian and military, emergency technicians must try to resuscitate victims until the medical examiner arrives and pronounces them dead.

It is understandable that every effort be made to save life and limb. But the efforts can be taken to ludicrous extremes, much to the chagrin of investigators. As a civilian policeman, Duncan once saw emergency personnel try to resuscitate a victim who was virtually decapitated.

Crime scene photographers, whose work is crucial to an effective investigation, also may be hampered by medical personnel.

Mike Duncan had gone to headquarters to check in after his first tour of the murder scene, and he was dismayed to see what had happened when he returned.

"The investigator walks in the house and sees paper, needles, hoses, everything lying all over the place. They make our job a lot harder," he said later.

For that reason, the crime scene photos, taken after the emergency personnel removed their equipment, could not accurately portray the original crime scene.

Duncan's concerns about unintentional sabotage of evidence by medical personnel were validated by what happened during removal of Sharon Sager's body:

A team of SBI agents who arrived the following day to collect and process evidence was told that blood had dripped from the body bag as Sharon's body was being carried out.

"This fact should be kept in mind while reviewing the results of the luminol examination" the agents were instructed. "The possibility of contamination (especially in the front entry area) does exist.

"Shoe tracks in blood were observed on the sidewalk outside the front door. Officers present stated that these tracks were made by those individuals who were removing the bodies of the victims from the residence."

While agents insist that contamination of the crime scene was kept to a minimum, it is nonetheless crucial to make note of all possible sources of contamination.

"You need the names, prints of everyone at the crime scene" said one investigator. "That was not done at this scene. I know, for example, medical personnel were not printed."

Years later, a former agent recalled other problems at the crime scene.

"First of all – and this happens on the outside too – uniform guys find the bodies. They're inside. They call CID. CID notifies NIS immediately. This is the biggest thing to hit Camp Lejeune.

"We have command interest and people are trying to be included. There were only certain people allowed in the house. But a lot of people showed up."

The first hours of the investigation centered on the quarters and immediate vicinity. Crucial evidence found downstairs included a bloody palm print discovered near the locking device on the sliding glass door adjacent to the couch where Sharon's body was discovered. The print was inside the drapes, within arm's reach of an adult standing beside the couch. No bloodstains were detected on the drapes.

A private detective who visited the quarters years later questioned why the bloody palm print on the sliding glass door was lifted instead of preserved.

"I'd have called housing maintenance and had them remove the whole door," he said. "You preserve evidence no matter what."

NIS agents also found a cigarette butt marked "Golden Lights" on the floor inside the front door. One bloodstained towel was seized from the downstairs bathroom; another from the playroom couch where Sharon Sager's body was found. There was evidence of blood on the sink board in the bathroom. On the floor beside the playroom couch, agents found a black knife sheath.

Upstairs, a black-handled fish scaling knife was found on

the closet side of the bed next to Tyler's body. The blade of the knife appeared to be covered with dried blood. But the area of the sheet directly under the knife was not bloodstained, indicating the blood had dried before the knife was dropped on the sheet.

A small quantity of blood was found on the light switch in Tyler's room and on two purses lying on the floor by the door. Scrapings were taken from drops of blood in the hallway outside the room where Tyler's body was found. Towels on the floor near the bathroom appeared to be stained with blood. A T-shirt, similarly stained, was also on the floor.

Autopsies were performed by Chief Pathologist Navy Cmdr. Steven Sohn at the Naval Regional Medical Center at Camp Lejeune on the afternoon of the day the bodies were discovered. Lt. Cmdr. John Almeida assisted. A routine re-examination was done two days later by Air Force forensic pathologist Lt. Col. Arnold R. Josselson.

Sharon, who was five feet, four inches tall and weighed 155 pounds, died from a neck wound that penetrated both carotid arteries, the trachea, esophagus and spinal column.

In addition to a defense wound on the left thumb, small abrasions of the upper lip and chin indicated she had struggled. The abrasions, which the report said might be fingernail marks, may have indicated the assailant's hand was placed over Sharon Sager's mouth.

There were additional wounds to the neck and a scalp hemorrhage which indicated either a blow to the head or the head striking against a fixed object.

"The large irregular nature of the fatal wound indicates some movement of either the knife and/or the assailant," the autopsy report would state. "The fatal wound track is approximately three to four inches long (deep) and the fact that the knife penetrated into a disc space indicates some force was involved in the thrust."

The direction of the wound was down, back and probably left to right. It measured six inches in length. A second wound, four inches in length penetrated several inches. It was also horizontal and located just above the fatal wound. Three superficial wounds measured between one and two inches in length.

The wound that killed Tyler Dash, who was the same height as his mother but 10 pounds lighter, was similar to those inflicted on her. It had "two terminations," indicating at least two thrusts.

Superficial defense wounds on both sides of the right hand, the back of the right elbow and the front of the left elbow indicated that Tyler, too, had struggled with his assailant. The direction of the fatal wound was "from the victim's left to right, front to back and down."

The body of Connie Smith, who was only five feet tall and weighed 120 pounds, had nine stabbing and incision wounds on the left side of her neck and head. The fatal neck wound was similar to those of the other victims. The knife entered below the left ear leaving an oblique wound with irregular edges. The direction of the six-inch-long wound was described as "from the victim's left to right, front to back and down."

Connie also received superficial horizontal and vertical wounds on the left side of her head and neck. Four of the wounds appeared to have been made after death. Small abrasions also were found on the right side of her neck and the front of her left shoulder. A hideous 19-inch wound in Connie's abdomen and chest was made after her death and was one continuous incision. It cut through her anus, vagina, uterus, left ureter, colon, liver, diaphragm and costal cartilage. The costal cartilage connects the ribs to the sternum.

"In spite of the strong sexual connotation at the scene of the crime, the post-mortem examination failed to reveal any evidence of sexual assault," the autopsy reported.

According to the doctors' estimates, the deaths occurred between 5:00 and 7:00 a.m, all within a 15-30 minute period.

CHAPTER 5

INITIAL STATEMENTS

After the murders, a communal shudder rippled over Camp Lejeune, particularly in Watkins Village. The occasional blood letting in base housing usually resulted from domestic discord fueled by alcohol. A ghoulish triple homicide was unthinkable.

"A Marine base is a controlled environment. There's violence, but not like on the outside," a former policeman and NIS agent explained.

Women whose husbands were overseas packed up children and returned to their parents' homes – or bought a handgun. Petless families shopped for Dobermans, and war veterans returned to the one-eye-open sleep pattern they'd perfected in Vietnam.

Top brass considered it imperative for morale that the killer be caught. Investigators, well aware of this, didn't take long to decide who that might be.

Almost immediately, Butch Smith had drawn the attention of neighbors and investigators with a variety of bizarre behaviors.

A teenage neighbor whose family knew the Smiths well said Butch came to her house at about 9:00 a.m. the morning of the murders. He was quite upset, she recalled.

"Why does blood come out of the ears of people who have their throats cut?" Butch asked. The neighbor ventured an explanation which Butch seemed to accept.

Butch then asked, "Why didn't he come after me when he came upstairs? He had to go right past me to get to the others and my door was open."

The neighbor could not answer that question. Butch remained in the neighbor's house for the rest of the morning, asking similar questions from time to time.

"It appeared to me that Butch was preoccupied with the question of blood and gore during the time he spent at my house, referring to the amount of blood he had seen and how cold the bodies were," the neighbor later told investigators.

An MP who was with Butch at a neighbor's quarters said at one point the boy slowly smiled and said, "I wish I could see my father's face right about now," then lapsed into silence.

The MP said Butch asked him what would happen to the killer if they caught him. Without waiting for a reply, Butch said he hoped whoever did it would be put in front of a firing squad and hanged at the same time.

Butch almost appeared to be trying to draw attention to himself. If that was his intent, he succeeded. He knew he had been singled out when the other children were taken from the scene and he was left behind.

He later said that while waiting in a neighbor's house, as he had been told to do, an agent came to the door. The agent gestured for Butch to accompany him outside.

Outside, the agent asked Butch, "Why?"

When Butch responded, "Why what?" the agent said, "Why did you do it?"

The agent warned Butch that he would be watched, then pointed at the scratches on the boy's face and wrist and predicted investigators would find Butch's skin under the victims' fingernails.

Later that day, Butch was taken to NIS headquarters and informally questioned. He was wearing the white shirt Susan Rodriguez had given him and the same jeans he had worn the day before. He was also wearing his "turf cleat" sneakers, the only shoes he owned apart from the pair of rubberized canvas combat-type boots and an outgrown pair of Little League baseball shoes.

Butch was asked to remove the jeans, he later said, and an MP left the room with them and returned to give them back a few minutes later.

Neither the jeans nor the shirt Butch had worn the day before and left wadded up on the floor by his bed had blood on them, according to NIS reports.

While at NIS headquarters, Butch was photographed to show the scratches on his cheek and wrist. They were the scratches that prompted the agent to conclude Butch's skin would be found under Sharon Sager's fingernails.

After he was photographed, Butch waited in a police vehicle while his mother was being interviewed in the provost marshal's office.

An MP who watched from a distance later said he was taken aback by Butch hanging outside the car window writhing, spitting and "doing everything but talking in tongues."

Mike Duncan agreed that Butch was acting strangely.

"This is what they were keying on: here's a kid who's an oddball. He was tall, he looked like Neanderthal man and they're saying this kid is mentally disturbed. He doesn't get along with anybody. He fights. His parents shipped him off. It was a kind of tunnel vision. They went with what they had."

Agents began interviewing Smith and Sager family members late in the afternoon of August 24.

Chris Sager, interviewed at 7:00 p.m., said he, Tommy, Butch and Tyler had been playing outside until 11:00 p.m. when Sharon called them inside. He and the other boys went upstairs and shot at targets with the new toy guns and watched the girls playing cards through the binoculars from Connie's bedroom window.

He stopped when Connie yelled at him and Butch to get out of her room.

Chris said the boys came downstairs at 12:45 a.m. and watched television until about 1:00 a.m. when Tommy went upstairs to bed. Butch followed about five minutes later.

The interviewer did not ask Chris where Tyler was during this time. It is likely Tyler went to bed first, in Lorrie's room.

Chris said he watched television alone until about 1:15 when he fell asleep on the floor. He said he woke at about 3:00 a.m. when he heard his mother talking to another woman.

Three days later, Chris was interviewed under hypnosis at the Naval Hospital by a clinical psychologist. His father, Fred Sager, consented to the interview but was not present while it was conducted.

Under hypnosis, Chris said he heard a conversation between his mother, his aunt and Gary Francis. Because Betty and Gary were at his trailer, it is likely Chris heard a phone conversation and subconsciously filled in the other voices. Or, perhaps, there was someone in the house and Chris, who was not particularly familiar with Gary's voice, merely supposed, subconsciously, that it was Gary he heard.

If Chris had been in the room with his mother, he would have seen the person she was talking to. But she may have gone into the kitchen to speak on the phone. Or Sharon may have stepped into the hallway to speak to a visitor so their voices wouldn't disturb the children.

What Chris said next, if accurate, would pinpoint the time of the murders. He said he woke at about 5:00 a.m. and went upstairs to Connie's room to sleep. At that time he saw his mother sleeping on the couch, her glasses perched on her head. The "babies" were sleeping on the floor by the far wall.

The interviewer did not ask Chris how he knew it was about 5:00 a.m. He did not ask the boy if he was wearing a watch or saw the kitchen clock or the wall clock in the play-room. But if Chris was correct about the time, Connie was already asleep on the living room couch when he went upstairs. Lorrie and a neighbor agreed she came in the house between 3:30 and 4:00 a.m.

(The interviewer, according to his notes, did not ask Chris whether he noticed Connie in the living room when he went upstairs.)

Also, if Chris was correct about the time, the murders had not yet taken place at 5:00 a.m. Sharon Sager was sleeping when her stepson went upstairs.

Because the children in the house agreed that Tommy woke Butch at about 7:00 a.m. and the coroner said the killings probably took place within a 20-30 minute period, Butch, if he were the killer, would have had little more than an hour to clean himself up, discard the evidence and return to bed.

Chris's brother Tommy also was interviewed on the 24th. Tommy had slept in the top bunk of the bed where Butch slept, and he was questioned closely about Butch.

How did the two get along?

"OK," Tommy said. "But sometimes I get on Butch's nerves and he gets mad."

The boy was then asked, "Are you afraid of Butch?"

"No," he replied.

"Are the other kids scared of Butch?"

"Connie is."

"Why?"

"Her and Butch always fight."

Twelve-year-old Deborah Dash had a more sanguine view of her cousin. She said Butch had a hot temper. That was why he had been sent to the camp. But he was nice to everyone and no one was scared of him.

She said the night of the murders, she, Lorrie and Connie had gone in the house with Butch and made popcorn at about 11:00 p.m. After eating the popcorn and watching television, the girls had returned to the car and Butch stayed inside, Debbie said.

She added that earlier on the day of the interview she had been talking to a teenage girl who lived next door. The girl told Debbie she had seen a man with a beard and mustache near the Smith quarters on the 23rd.

The girl confirmed Debbie's description of the bearded man as did another child. Based on the statements, NIS created three composite drawings. Apart from the mustaches and beards, the drawings showed rather nondescript features. As a result, witnesses said the drawings resembled a number of men, including several construction workers, a civilian hospital employee and the husband of a female staff sergeant.

Gary Francis also was interviewed the day of the murders. He told investigators he had picked Betty up at about 3:00 p.m. Sunday at the nursing home where she worked. They planned to go out to dinner and a movie that evening.

They went to Francis' residence and spent a couple of hours playing cards with three of his friends. During this time, Francis borrowed 50 dollars from one of the men, but had the lender make the check out to Betty so she could get it cashed at a nearby bar where she sometimes worked.

Betty used 20 dollars of the money to buy beer and frozen pizzas for the card-players.

Francis showered and changed. At about 5:30 p.m., he and Betty drove to Kentucky Court so Betty too could shower and change for the evening.

While Betty was getting ready, Francis chatted with Sharon. He said the children, including Butch and Connie, were all running in and out of the residence.

Francis told investigators Butch was wearing a maroon football jersey and blue Levis with what appeared to be acid stains on one leg.

Betty gave Sharon some money to buy dinner for the children, before she and Francis left at about 6:30 and drove to a Sneads Ferry restaurant. They stayed in the restaurant until about 8:30, then took a half-hour walk on the beach.

At 9:30, they returned to Francis' trailer, having stopped for gas on the way home. Francis said they did not go to a movie because he did not have enough money. No one was there when they arrived. The couple watched television until about 11:00. Francis was feeling sick at his stomach so Betty went to a convenience store across the street to buy some milk.

"She was gone only 10-15 minutes and when she returned

54

she said she had called her residence and spoke with Sharon and everything was fine," Francis said.

Betty called from the store because the phone in Francis' trailer was not working.

At about 12:15 a.m., Betty and Francis went to bed together. He said he awoke about 5:30, went to the bathroom then returned to bed. He awoke again at 7:40, woke Betty and got ready for work. They left the trailer at about 8:30. Francis planned to drop Betty off and then report to work.

Instead, they arrived at Betty's apartment only to be drawn into the horror and confusion that followed the discovery of the bodies.

CHAPTER 6

KNIVES AND ACCUSATIONS

Confusion over the knife alleged to be the murder weapon began the day the bodies were discovered.

When Betty was questioned on the evening of August 24, before she had reason to believe Butch was a suspect, she was shown the knife found in the bed with Tyler's body. She said it did not belong to her or her children.

Betty would consistently insist that the fish knife she owned had a wooden, not black plastic, handle. In any event, a wooden-handle knife also identified in evidence lists as a "fish knife" was seized from the quarters. The plastic-handle knife was a common type of knife, literally sold by the dozens in the base exchange.

Butch, even more than Betty, seemed to have been confused about which knife was implicated in the killings.

The wooden-handle fish knife Butch usually carried in his tackle box was of lesser quality than the sharp plastic-handle knife found it Tyler's bed. He told agents the black-handle knife was kept in the kitchen and he had used it the night of the murders to cut salami.

Agents began to refer to the plastic-handle knife as "Butch's knife." But Butch assumed the knife they referred to as the murder weapon was the wooden-handle fish knife.

Butch did own several knives, including a pocket knife and a Buck knife his dad had given him. But the kitchen knives didn't belong to him any more than they belonged to any other member of the household.

Chris, when asked if there were any hunting knives in the house, said there was a large fishing knife kept on the counter in the kitchen. He said Butch owned only pocket knives.

Agents never showed Butch the alleged murder knife.

A sheath for the black-handle knife, with a broken belt loop, was found near the couch where Sharon Sager died. Butch said he last saw the sheath on the kitchen counter which divided the kitchen from the playroom.

Agents thought it significant that the sheath belonging to "Butch's knife" was found near Sharon Sager's body. The implication was that the killer removed the knife from the sheath before killing the woman.

But witnesses who remembered seeing the black-handle knife said it was either in or next to the sink – unsheathed. There were no usable fingerprints on the sheath. More significantly, there was no blood.

A red camping knife as well as a piece of driftwood and a hammer were seized from Butch's room and tested for blood. None was found.

The outside doorknob to Butch's room had bloodstains on it and was taken by investigators. The blood later was found to be consistent with Tyler's blood type.

The spigot handle and sink board in the downstairs bathroom also showed blood but of insufficient quantity to be identified. No blood or usable prints were found on the front door knob. Also unusable were the bloody fingerprints found inside the playroom toybox and under the stair banister.

Small spots of Connie's blood were found in the second

floor hallway, but there was no blood found on the cake of soap in the upstairs bath or around the sink fixtures.

Indications of blood were detected on the light switch in the room where Tyler died.

Garbage was picked up in Watkins Village the morning of the killings, just before the bodies were discovered. Agents subsequently considered whether the killer might have discarded evidence in a garbage can. Had they considered this earlier, agents could have seized the slow-moving garbage truck and analyzed its contents.

Realizing the oversight, an agent said, NIS considered searching the landfill but decided the effort would be futile.

Of all the puzzling pieces of evidence related to the crime, the knife left in the bed with Tyler became one of the most difficult to explain. Why did the killer, who made efforts to clean up the crime scene, who left so little evidence behind, leave the murder weapon?

Some investigators suspected there was a second knife. A knife that was removed from the scene by the killer. If there was a second weapon, the killer may have forgotten he used the filet knife. Or he may have forgotten where he left it and decided not to take the time to search for it.

One element that would complicate reconstruction of the crime was the matter of the dried blood on the knife left next to Tyler's body. Because the sheet beneath the knife was not stained, the blood – Connie's – had already dried on the blade when the knife was placed there.

Those who would come to believe that Butch was the killer contend he dropped it near Tyler's body before returning to his room. But that wouldn't explain a fingerprint the FBI found on the knife handle. A fingerprint that turned out not to be Butch's.

Lab reports concerning the knife later also would reveal the presence of a nylon fiber embedded in the dried blood.

Great significance would be given to a pair of girl's underpants found in Lorrie's room near the head of the bed where Tyler's body lay. Lorrie tentatively identified the underpants, part of a scattering of girl's clothing, as Connie's.

Because Connie's bloodstained shorts, but no underpants, were found near her body, investigators conjectured that the killer had removed the underpants from the girl's body, carried them upstairs and dropped them by the bed when Tyler was killed.

Yet, no blood was found on the underpants. Could the killer, after slashing two people to death, remove the girl's shorts, staining them liberally with blood, then remove her underpants without staining them at all?

Perhaps Connie was not wearing underpants.

Or, perhaps, the killer removed Connie's underpants and took them with him. It is not unusual in sexual homicides for a killer to take an item belonging to the victim from the murder scene.

Connie's underpants took on special significance in view of developments that began the day of the murders. Clearly, Connie's death was a sexual homicide. And that afternoon agents began to suspect that Butch had had an incestuous relationship with his younger sister.

Special Agent Michael Paul interviewed 17-year-old Sherry Nonceville* at her home, near the Smith apartment. Sherry's sister, Marsha*, was Lorrie's best friend. The two girls often spent the night with each other.

Sherry told the agent that one day in early August she was sitting on the steps of her residence when Connie came over. Connie sat down and asked Sherry if she might spend the night with her because Marsha was spending the night with Lorrie.

"I explained to Connie that I would prefer if she did not spend the night with me as I was too old and did not care to have her at my house," Sherry told Agent Paul.

Sherry said Connie then asked, "Why are brothers so mean?" Sherry told her that being mean was normal for most brothers and not to worry. Sherry said Connie then told her she was afraid of her brother.

Sherry said about two weeks later she spoke to Connie once more, this time in the Noncevilles' kitchen. Again Connie asked if she could spend the night with Sherry as Marsha was spending the night with Lorrie.

According to Sherry, Connie then said that she was afraid of her brother and that sometimes they wrestled with one another. Sherry told Connie she had to get up early the following morning and preferred that Connie not spend the night.

The day after the murders, August 25, an agent interviewed Tyler's father, Dennis Dash. According to the agent's notes, Dash said his son had called him Saturday. Tyler told his father he wasn't happy. He complained about "the girls' sexual acts and the wildness of the kids."

Dash said Tyler asked him to call back Monday. When he did, Dash said, he learned of the murders.

The agent's notes fail to explain which girls or what "sexual acts" Tyler was referring to. But Dash made no mention of Butch.

Six days later, Dash would be interviewed again by another agent. This time, Dash said he had seen Tyler when the boy was in New York visiting his grandparents the week before the murders. Dash said Tyler had seemed happy and didn't complain about any particular problems.

Dash said he spoke to Tyler by phone on August 22, after Tyler had returned to Camp Lejeune. Tyler told his father he was unhappy with the situation at the Smith residence.

"He specifically complained about Butch's conduct and use of foul language," Dash told the agent.

Dash said Tyler told him "he had caught Butch in bed twice with Connie Smith." According to Tyler, he had told his mother about the incidents and she said she would tell Betty.

Tyler said his mother had gone through his wallet and taken Dash's phone numbers from him. He told his father that they were moving to Fayetteville to live with Sharon Sager's in-laws.

The boy asked his father to call his mother and tell her that he should be allowed to call Dash, collect, at any time. Dash told the agent that the conversation ended "on a friendly note."

In a third interview, Dash said that when Tyler and Debbie had visited him in New York, Tyler said he was not happy living at Camp Lejeune with his mother. He said Tyler had told him Butch was treating him badly.

Three weeks earlier, Tyler said, he had walked in on Butch, "who was sleeping with his sister Connie."

But three weeks earlier had been August 1. Butch did not return from the Eckerd Camp until Aug. 11.

Questioned about the discrepancy, Dash said Tyler told him the incident happened just before the Smiths and Sagers traveled to Springville, N.Y. However, Butch was home less than 24 hours between returning from the camp and the departure for New York.

Dash's statements would be reinforced, however, by a similar accusation made against Butch on September 3 by Fred Sager, Sharon's husband. Sager told an NIS agent that he had called Sharon from Alaska on the "10th or 12th" of August. She told him that something terrible was going to happen at the Smith residence. Betty was using dangerous drugs, Sharon said, and Butch and Connie were having sexual relations with each other. Sager said his wife told him she wanted to get her children away.

Sager said he told Sharon to take their children to New York. Betty later said that neither Sharon nor her husband said one word to her about those accusations and that there had been ample opportunity for both of them to confide in her.

And, on August 10, Butch was at camp and Sharon hadn't seen him for years. The family brought him home on August 11 and left for New York the next day, the 12th.

Betty later would say that it was painfully difficult for her to understand why any family member could have had such suspicions and not told her. And it was inconceivable that her outspoken, sometimes mercilessly critical, sister would not have told her if she suspected that Butch was having sex with Connie.

"My sister would have said, you get your ass home, stop working nights and take care of these kids," Betty said.

CHAPTER 7

INTERROGATION

Butch's mother took him to the Provost Marshal's Office on Tuesday morning, August 25, to be interviewed. The rights waiver he signed said he was suspected of the murders of Sharon Sager, Tyler Dash and Connie Smith.

He saw Tyler's father as he was escorted through the reception area.

"You ought to fry in hell, you little son of a bitch!" he later recalled Dash shouting at him.

Butch was interviewed by Special Agent Mike Jones. Also present were Special Agent Deborah Cobb and a Navy doctor. The doctor was there, according to Jones, in view of Butch's age and "just in case there was some emotional outbreak or something of that nature."

Jones was an experienced agent but had little formal training in interrogation. During a later court hearing, Jones explained, "I received a small block of instruction 22 years ago, when I was going through basic school, but none since then."

Butch was not intimidated by his situation. He readily offered his statement, even chiming in as the agent read him his rights. He described Sunday's events in a fairly straightforward manner, until the time he went to bed. At 2:30 a.m., he said, after getting up to go to the bathroom and returning, he thought he heard footsteps and called out, "Who's there?"

When he got no answer, he walked to the top of the stairs carrying a billy club. The footsteps stopped, he returned to bed and again heard footsteps.

Several times he got up after hearing footsteps, asked who was there and then returned to bed.

When he heard the footsteps coming up the stairs, he grew frightened and got the .410 shotgun his stepfather had given him out of the closet. The gun was unloaded; the shells downstairs.

He went to the top of the stairs, flipped on the light but saw no one. He then heard three thuds that he took to be someone on the stairs. He went back to his room and shut the door.

Tommy, he said in the statement, was asleep on the top bunk through all of this.

Butch said he then was awakened by noises again and saw that his door was open. He got up, shut it and went back to sleep. The same thing happened again, he said, and then once more.

The third time, Butch said, he got up, went downstairs, put the shotgun in the hall closet and went back to bed, where he slept until awakened by Tommy.

Later, Jones described the interview as calm and congenial. But Betty, who was under enormous strain and sensed what she felt was a contemptuous attitude on the part of investigators, had a different view. She said Jones was hostile to her as well as Butch.

"I felt like I was being talked to by the Gestapo," she later recalled. "He'd ask questions and wouldn't wait for answers. He just kept throwing question after question. Half the time I didn't know what he was saying."

During the latter part of the six-hour interview, which included several breaks, Butch's natural father, who had just arrived, sat listening. His presence, while well-intended, only added to the stress he was under, Butch said later.

Agents knew immediately that Butch's statement was ridiculous. The shotgun had not been in Butch's room that night. It was gathering dust in the downstairs hall closet.

In later statements given by Butch, the nonexistent billy club would become a baseball bat and then be scrapped altogether.

Some agents believed Butch lied to cover for committing murder. But others considered another possibility. A boy who wove fantasies about his own physical toughness, a boy who'd been ordered by his father to protect his mother and sisters, might not be able to deal with the reality that he had slept while his sister was slain.

While Butch was being interviewed, agents from the North Carolina State Bureau of Investigation were at the Kentucky Court crime scene at the request of NIS. They processed latent fingerprints and visible bloodstains in addition to conducting luminol tests to find blood that could not be seen.

The chemical luminol can detect invisible footprints, palm prints, splatter patterns or wipe marks remaining from an attempt to clean up spilled blood. The test is done in the dark because the chemical causes the blood to emit a bluish-white luminescence.

It can be an eerie experience. Former SBI Agent Stephen R. Jones recalls being at the scene of an elderly woman's murder at 4 a.m., tracking the killer's glowing footprints all over the victim's house.

At the Kentucky Court crime scene, Jones was the latent fingerprint examiner. SBI chemist Brenda Bissette analyzed blood. The two worked through the night, coordinating their tasks to the intermittent darkness needed by the agents doing the luminol tests.

Agents found a few luminol reactions in the front entryway; a few drop-like reactions in front of the sofa where Connie died; and a few drop-like reactions next to the sliding glass door at the end of the couch where Sharon Sager died.

Luminol examination of the rest of the house failed to reveal any blood patterns which had not already been visually observed. No blood was found in Butch's room.

A pair of green sateen trousers found on the floor of Butch's room was later determined to have a minute trace of human blood on them. Investigators considered it unlikely the garment was related to the crime, however.

Had they been worn by the killer, they would have revealed more than minute traces. And, although Butch would say he may have touched Tyler and subsequently wiped his hand on the back of his leg, many witnesses would verify Butch was wearing jeans – not the green trousers – the morning the bodies were discovered.

From an investigative standpoint, the duplex was extraordinarily "clean." The blood at the scene was almost entirely with the victims' bodies.

Jones did find numerous fingerprints and palm prints "of value for identification." Many of the prints would fail to fulfill their potential value, though. Their sources would never be identified.

It was exacting – and exhausting – work. Midway between midnight and dawn, Jones drove Bissette back to the courthouse in Garner. She had left her car there and driven to Jacksonville with Jones after testifying in a court case. After dropping Bissette off, Jones slept in the front seat of his car in the courthouse parking lot, too weary to drive on to Raleigh.

Jones was aware that Butch Smith was a suspect. He also knew it was not his job to decide whether Butch or anyone else should be indicted.

"I was just one of the hired hands there to do a job," he said. "I've always wanted to do the job like I'd want it done if I were the victim or the suspect. Go in with an open mind and keep an open mind. Try to focus on what was actually there and not what could have been."

But Jones did have his own ideas.

"My initial impression was that Butch could have done it. I felt that very strongly. But our evidence didn't show that."

CHAPTER 8

FUNERAL

Three days after the murders, Betty Smith's family was placed in protective custody and moved from Gary Francis' trailer to the Hostess House, a motel on base for military families in transit. Kitchen facilities are included in each unit.

The move served to isolate Butch and the family for observation. Betty was even accompanied by agents on her trips to the commissary. She resented the intrusion and often tried to evade the agents.

Fred Sager, who had arrived from Alaska, stayed two nights with Betty and the children in the pair of adjoining suites assigned to the family. During this time, Betty later said, Sager did not tell her what he would tell NIS the following week: that Sharon had told him of an incestuous relationship between Butch and Connie.

An NIS agent assigned to observe the family said Butch, who knew the agent, greeted him in the motel parking lot on

August 27. The boy sat in the agent's car and watched a passing truck convoy. He wanted "to see if their bodies are in the back of the trucks," the agent later reported Butch saying.

Butch told the agent he couldn't stand to be in the room with a body but, in his sister's case, he would like to see her guts put back in and her body sewed up. He asked the agent who could give permission for such a viewing.

The agent was about to ask Butch why something like that would interest him. He was interrupted by Lorrie running up to the car saying her mother and stepfather, who had been brought back to North Carolina because of the murders, were having a fight inside their Hostess House suite. Butch jumped out of the car, the agent said, to break up the fight. The agent followed and brought the situation under control.

Butch made several similarly macabre remarks after the slayings. But while indicative of disturbed thinking, they also showed limited knowledge of the crimes.

Connie's body was frequently described in newspaper stories as "disemboweled." But photos taken at the scene show her viscera were not actually removed from the body cavity.

Fights between Betty and Staff Sgt. Jim Smith soon would be limited to bitter memories. They had but one more ceremony to attend as a couple.

"We traveled to New York together for the funeral and then it was over," Betty said.

The funeral was especially stressful for Butch because both his natural father and stepfather were present.

"I was confused over who to call 'Dad,' " Butch later told his lawyer. "I called my real father 'Jim' but my dad pulled me outside the funeral home and told me to cut it out."

Betty had not intended that Connie have an open casket. She was so distraught at the time, she could not later recollect signing the form indicating that preference.

Betty said the funeral director later told her he had been surprised at her decision to have an open casket. He said the bodies had arrived in such a poor condition he never would have recommended it.

Butch was nearly as miserable as his mother. And much

more restless. Before the funeral was over, his dad sent him home with a sympathetic aunt.

Butch went to visit the graves with his stepfather the next day. When the boy began to sob, Smith told him to let it all come out.

They were not aware they were being videotaped by NIS agents.

CHAPTER 9

ERRORS

Evidence seized from the murder scene included: a second fish-scaling knife; one baseball bat; one .410 Mossberg shotgun taken from the downstairs hall closet; five additional knives; a diving knife from Butch's room; 20 additional baseball bats and a rifle.

The accumulation of baseball bats was a tribute to the popularity of Little League, girls' softball and baseball in the Smith household.

Among the myriad potential weapons seized from the quarters, there were no bayonets, a deficiency that would later be significant. Apart from the grisly fish knife, none of the potential weapons appeared to bear blood.

A search of the duplex on August 30 produced a bloody fingerprint inside a toybox found in the playroom.

The following day, surfaces in the duplex were processed with ninhydrin latent fingerprint spray. Rugs were vacuumed for fibers, hairs or other evidence. Neither procedure proved productive.

The same day, an agent discovered what appeared to be a bloody fingerprint under the stair banister. The agent who discovered it was dismayed that it had not been found earlier and feared the print might have been inadvertently smudged during the week since the crimes had been committed.

At any crime scene, there are literally thousands of possibilities for error, oversight and contamination. Some contamination, even by investigators, is inevitable. It is unreasonable to expect a flawless investigation from any agency.

But when there is contamination of a crime scene by an agent, it is especially demoralizing. And embarrassing.

One agent arrived for an early evidence-collecting session and discovered a novice agent using the upstairs toilet.

"Why don't you come in and have a picnic?" the agent sarcastically asked the younger man. "You don't come to a crime scene and smoke or chew or eat. What do you think you might have flushed down there?"

The destruction of a set of footprints at the crime scene was cited by several agents as an example of carelessness.

"It was a great embarrassment," a former NIS agent recalled. "An agent told Sleeper there were boot impressions in the sand outside the patio door. He was told to get the footprint. The dumb shit didn't even take pictures. Anybody who'd been to the FBI Academy would know to take a plaster cast.

"He takes a shovel, picks the footprint up and, of course, it falls to pieces. At NIS everybody was laughing about it. The boss really got mad about it."

One agent drew a caricature of his co-worker haphazardly wielding a shovel. He left his artwork on the chagrined investigator's desk.

The official report says: "Two partial latent footprints were found in the dirt immediately adjacent to the patio at the rear of the residence. Due to the texture of the soil and quality of the footprints, no attempt was made to obtain plaster-of-Paris molds. The two footprints were carefully dug from the ground and sprayed with clear plastic lacquer."

The destroyed footprint may have been insignificant. Or it may have been very significant.

A "footwear impression" was found on the cushion covering Connie's body. It would appear the cushion was on the floor when the killer stepped on it. Investigators would speculate the killer then placed the cushion over her body as a gesture of remorse.

Investigators surmised the impression was made by someone wearing a re-soled combat boot. Marines are allowed to have their boots customized in this way and many choose to do so. Such a sole leaves a footprint resembling a series of interlocking Ws.

There were no such boots in the Smith house. Butch, Tyler and the Sager boys usually wore sneakers. The soles of the green combat-type boots found in Butch's room did not match the footprint.

If the destroyed patio footprint was consistent with the impression on the cushion, it would indicate the killer had looked in or been admitted through the patio door before committing the murders.

In another example of carelessness, A CID agent recalled finding evidence from the crime scene in the parking lot of the Provost Marshal's Office, located downstairs from NIS offices.

"Somebody had dropped it. It wasn't of any value but it stuck in my mind," he said.

Explanations for the errors center on a simple lack of experience.

"The resident crime scene officer was basically self-taught. A former navy officer, meticulous, but he'd never seen a homicide crime scene," a former agent said. "Most people haven't seen a scene like that – unless they've been in combat."

Another agent characterized investigators as "totally overawed. Trying to do a good job but unprepared to deal with it."

"Incompetents led by the egotistical," was one former agent's scathing assessment.

The agent, who admitted having little admiration for Sleeper, said NIS should have allowed the FBI to assist in the case more fully from the beginning.

Cooperation was impeded, he claims, by the animosity that exists between NIS and every other Department of Defense investigative agency.

"Why did the physical evidence go to the SBI instead of the FBI? Three people killed, the SBI had no jurisdiction. Why not send it to the best lab and get the fastest results?"

Mike Duncan disagrees vehemently. "The people who processed the scene were well-trained. The procedures are the same whether you've seen one homicide or a thousand. And we brought in both the SBI and the FBI to take advantage of their expertise.

"Just because they're FBI doesn't mean they're God's gift to investigators," Duncan snapped.

It was the FBI's prerogative whether to assume the investigation. The bureau elected to monitor only.

It was more than a week after the killings when Special Agent Michael Paul, assisted by a platoon of MPs, swept through the woods abutting the housing area. They directed special attention to the places agents had been told were frequented by neighborhood teens. Coordinates, marked with flags, were set up to facilitate the search.

"We spent 20 hours searching the area," Paul recalled. "We found warm beer, pornographic books and cigarettes. But no weapons and no drugs. And no *Soldier of Fortune* magazine."

It was significant that no issues of the mercenary magazine were found. Agents, recognizing the homicides indicated a murderous expertise, theorized that Butch had acquired that skill by reading *Soldier of Fortune*.

During the search of the woods, Paul, an Army reservist, wore fatigues in lieu of the standard suit and tie.

Because of the incident, Paul said, when he later fell into disfavor with NIS, he would be characterized by his critics as a "psycho who ran around Lejeune in battle dress."

On September 4, base maintenance workers opened the sewer pipes leading to the quarters. Plumbing fixtures within the residence were "activated" to flush items from the pipes to a nearby manhole. Investigators thought the killer may have disposed of bloody clothing by flushing it. A maintenance supervisor said that if a garment had been thrown in one of the toilets, it would have plugged it up. Nothing pertinent was discovered in the pipes.

A curious piece of possible evidence would not be discovered until more than a month after the killings. Paul, who had not been involved in the initial seizures, was at the quarters to meet Betty and a Marine captain from the base legal office.

Paul was there to let Betty into the apartment to get some of her personal effects. While he waited, he pensively walked through the quarters, as he had done several times before, on the chance he might spot some overlooked piece of evidence. Clotted blood was still on the floor where Connie had died. Fine spatters of blood still traced across the ceiling.

For the thousandth time he asked himself why investigators had not been able to find any bloody clothes.

He opened the closet in the downstairs hall and was astounded to see an olive-drab CBR suit. The garment, which zips up the front like a jumpsuit, is issued to military personnel as protection against chemical, biological and radiological elements.

"The first thing I thought was, this would be the perfect thing for the killer to put on," Paul said.

The agent pulled the suit off the hanger and looked at it more closely. There appeared to be a rust-colored stain down the front of the suit, next to the zipper.

Paul was amazed that agents had not already seized the suit. He did not discuss his find with Betty or the Marine lawyer. But he did take the suit back to NIS, put it in an evidence bag, log it in and ship it off to the SBI lab.

Paul said the lab determined the stain was, indeed, human blood but of insufficient quantity for further analysis.

The suit did not appear on NIS lists of items seized from the crime scene, although a diving suit, a raincoat and a windbreaker were taken from the same closet by another agent.

Betty later said she could not recall such a garment but her husband had owned a variety of military surplus gear.

The crime scene was officially "sealed," the duplex boarded up, on September 11.

CHAPTER 10

EYEWITNESS

S pecial Agent Carl St. John* found himself cruising through Kentucky Court even when off duty. Although he had walked through the grim scene the day of the murders, for the most part, his responsibilities had entailed taking statements from witnesses.

Like the other agents, St. John hoped that one of the evidence-seizure sweeps through the duplex would unearth that one illuminating item, something to clear the murky waters.

He did not believe Butch was the killer. And it was becoming uncomfortably plain that his thoughts on the matter were not pleasing to his boss, Arnold Sleeper.

As he was standing on the sidewalk in front of 6080A, a tousle-haired teenage girl wearing frayed-edge shorts and no shoes came up to him.

"Are you an NIS guy?" she asked, shading her eyes with her hand.

St. John smiled. In their suits, ties, trench coats and "FBI shoes," agents weren't too difficult to spot on the Marine base.

"Sure am. How can I help you?"

"I thought you might like to know. My brother saw that lady get killed in that house." The girl nodded toward 6080A.

The agent continued to smile, but he began to register details of the girl's voice and demeanor. The girl was smiling too. A polite smile, devoid of coyness.

"What's your name, Miss?"

"Katie Davis*. My brother that saw everything is Bobby." Bobby Davis*. The name was familiar but, for a moment, St. John couldn't remember why.

"Where do you live, Katie?"

"Right across the street." The teenager pointed to the duplex directly across from the Smith quarters. Two younger children were standing inside the garage door, nearly lost in a jungle of toys, lawn furniture and recycled shipping cartons.

Bobby Davis, St. John remembered, was the five-year-old who had spent the night in the Smith quarters on August 23. He was a friend of Scotty and Skippy Sager. He had slept on the floor of the playroom where Sharon died, on the cushions with the Sager children.

Investigators had assumed all three little boys had slept through the bloody rampage. Maybe not.

St. John assured Katie he would like, very much, to talk to Bobby. But first he must talk to the children's mother.

Katie shook her head. "She won't like that I told you. She really went nuts when she found out there was people killed in that house where Bobby was. She don't even like anybody to talk about it around Bobby."

The agent told Katie she needn't worry. Every effort would be made to see that her mother and brother were disturbed as little as possible.

Katie waved as she sauntered off at a self-consciously slow pace. She probably was fighting an impulse to break and run, St. John thought. She couldn't wait to hear her friends' reactions to her conversation with the "NIS guy."

He forced himself to suppress a surge of optimism. Bobby

Davis might be able to shed a little light on those murky waters. But his mother's cooperation was nearly as crucial as the child's.

Kentucky Court was a communal playground for the children who lived in the duplexes. Sorting out tricycles, wagons and doll strollers abandoned on the circular sidewalk was a day's-end ritual, as were occasional youthful squabbles over ownership.

Sara Davis* had ample experience in sorting toys and arbitrating children's disputes. She was the mother of eight, including Katie, Bobby and a three-month-old baby.

Soon after the Sagers' arrival at Camp Lejeune, Sara had noticed the two rambunctious preschoolers visiting at Betty Smith's house directly across the court. They had eagerly drawn Bobby into their play and the three soon were bouncing from one set of quarters to the other.

The court had been considerably quieter while the Smiths and their house guests were away in New York, and Bobby had been delighted when the Sager youngsters returned. No sooner had Skippy and Scotty tumbled from the car Saturday than they were at the Davis house, urging Bobby's mother to allow him to spend the night at the Smiths'.

Maybe tomorrow, she responded.

She had met Sharon Sager only briefly but she had known Betty Smith for some time. Although she had heard rumors of Betty's relationships with men other than her husband, she nonetheless considered her a caring mother.

Lorrie and Katie were good friends too, so the Sager relatives seemed a natural addition to the Davis' circle of acquaintances.

If there was dissension between Butch and his cousin Tyler, Sara was unaware of it. Years later, she would discredit Butch's recollection of a fierce fight with Tyler in front of the Smith quarters on Sunday, August 23. It couldn't have happened without her knowledge, she insisted. "When something like that happened, everybody on the court knew it."

But she hesitated to permit Bobby to spend the night at the Smiths' that Saturday. Bobby was a quiet, sensitive child who had been plagued lately by bad dreams. He had told his mother that in his dream a man was after him.

"He has a knife," Sara recalled her frightened son telling her when he described his nightmares.

Adding to her uneasiness was a letter she had received from her Marine husband, serving an unaccompanied tour overseas.

"He wrote and said he'd been dreaming that something was going on," she recalled. "He wrote that I should keep Bobby close."

And there had been another, seemingly silly, incident that would later take on eerie import. As something of a lark, Sara had consulted a psychic. The self-proclaimed seer, who used cards as a fortune-telling device, foresaw "a bad thing fixing to happen with a young child."

Sara said she was told the bad thing was somehow related to a representative of authority.

"I know it sounds crazy now," she said of the ominous incidents.

On Sunday, August 23, the small Sagers persisted in their requests that Bobby spend the night with them, and Sara finally relented.

In the evening, Davis customarily would spend a few moments looking over the court from the balcony window of her sons' room. The duplex balconies served the same purpose as rural front porches during times past. From that vantage, she, like others in the complex, would greet a passing neighbor, see who was home and who was not and take note of which children were playing in which yard. During the summer months, it was not unusual for youngsters to be outside until midnight.

That Sunday, Sara noticed an extraordinary number of unfamiliar cars parked in the court. "The court was full, like somebody was having a party. I'd never seen the court so full of cars."

She had difficulty sleeping that night. At about 3:30 a.m. Monday, she was in the kitchen feeding her new baby and was surprised to see the court still full of cars and the lights on at the Smith apartment. She noted lights were on in the two upstairs front rooms. And a softer light came from the living room, as if the light were spilling over from the hallway.

She then recalled that the girls had planned to sleep in the red station wagon pulled up to the front door. She assumed the lights had been left on for them.

Sara also noted an unfamiliar dark sedan parked in front of the Smith apartment. Preoccupied with her youngest child, it did not strike her then that Bobby was in that house.

At about 5:30, Davis drove a stranded friend to work as she had agreed to do the night before. When she returned at 6:00, the same dark sedan was still in front of the Smiths'.

Shortly thereafter, Davis walked to a neighbor's house for a cup of coffee. The neighbor walked Davis to the door as she was leaving. The two women noticed across the yard the emergency vehicles, military police and anxious onlookers that had materialized during their coffee visit.

Sara walked toward her quarters and asked one of the somber assembly what had happened. Someone said "homicide." Distracted by the extraordinary goings-on, she took several more steps before being struck by the word's dreadful significance and the horrifying recollection of where Bobby was.

She began to scream, "My baby! My baby" and was forcibly restrained by investigators from entering the blocked-off entrance to the house. What seemed an endless parade of small, silent children were being carried from the Smith's quarters to ambulances. It was impossible to tell whether they were injured or merely immobilized by frightening, unfathomable events.

A frantic Sara was reassured that her son was unharmed. She accompanied him to the naval hospital where it was confirmed that Bobby had suffered no physical injuries. The only outward sign of Bobby's experience was an uncharacteristic hyperactivity. It was as though he thought being still for even a moment would place him in danger.

"That day, him and the other little boys went 160 miles-per-hour," his mother later recalled. "You couldn't slow them down."

She would remember Butch's behavior that day. "I do not believe that child did that," she said, referring to Butch being named a suspect. "I knew the boy before. And the way he went off and was emotional after that, and when he found out Connie was dead tried to get back in the house. He cared about Connie too much."

Within hours of the discovery of the bodies, Sara learned that Bobby had not slept through the night's horrific events. From less than eight feet away, Bobby had seen Sharon Sager murdered.

But his mother was too distraught to deal with Bobby's important role in the investigation.

Had Katie not volunteered information to Special Agent St. John, Bobby's knowledge of the murders might have remained a family secret.

Davis resisted NIS efforts to question her son, fearing he would be further traumatized. She finally agreed that 16-year-old Katie could act as intermediary between her brother and investigators.

Bright, confident Katie had often cared for her younger brothers and sisters. She was especially fond of Bobby and he trusted her utterly. Although sympathetic to the Smith family's tragedy, the young woman found it exciting to be part of such a momentous investigation.

In late September, NIS agents arranged to videotape Katie questioning Bobby at their home. Katie coaxed her brother into talking by offering to take him to an upcoming fair. Bobby asked if he would be allowed to ride whatever he wished, even the bumper cars.

"You can get on the bumper cars, the merry-go-round. You can win some stuffed animals. You can play basketball. You can do all kinds of things. Anything you want to do," she assured him.

In exchange for a trip to the fair, Bobby was to tell his sister about what happened at the Smith's house.

Struggling to find words, Bobby said he saw a man go in the kitchen. Only a counter separated the kitchen from the room where the three little boys were lying on sofa cushions.

He said he was sleeping when the man entered the house. "And then I woke up and looked why the light was on."

He said the man rummaged through drawers in the kitchen as though looking for something. "He just looked in there a long, long, long, long time."

"Did he do anything to Tyler's mom?" Katie asked.

"Tyler's mom already killed."

"Who killed her?"

"That man. In her head like this," Bobby made jabbing motions at his sister's head.

"He cut her forehead?"

"All over. Where you can't see her face."

"Did you see him do it?"

"Yeah."

The child described a man with a beard – a man he said he had not seen before.

His anxiety at recalling the events was betrayed by a recurring stammer and his difficulty in describing them resulted from the normal limitations of a five-year-old's vocabulary. He used objects, including a toothbrush, to try to describe the arrangement of the Smith house. He showed his sister that the man had gone upstairs.

"Where was Butch at?" Katie asked.

"Butch? He was upstairs. He's still alive?"

"Yeah. He's still alive. Did the man see Butch?"

"Nope," Bobby replied.

"Did the man see you?"

"If I was upstairs he would have saw me."

"But he didn't see you."

"He didn't see Butch either," Bobby said. "I believe Butch was downstairs or upstairs. I don't know where he was. I didn't see him. I just saw the man."

Bobby's conviction that Butch was not the killer was confirmed by his body language. When he spoke of "the man" he stuttered. He had no such speech impediment when he spoke of Butch.

Katie persisted in trying to get a more specific description of the man. But the child became frustrated trying to describe the colors of the killer's clothing and hair, in part, because he was not yet sure of the names of colors.

Katie tried to help by asking him to relate what he'd seen to the colors of items around him. She had him stand on a bed in an attempt to describe the man's height, and asked him to compare the man's bulk to that of his father and other men he knew.

She asked Bobby if he had "played possum" when the man came in the house. Bobby said he had been "pretend" sleeping, but believed Sharon Sager really had been sleeping because she was softly snoring.

Bobby did not know how the man left, just that he did. "Know why he left?" he asked Katie.

"Why?"

"Cause it was gettin' real morning time. When people come back and go outside and play and all that. That's why he left."

During another videotaped interview, Katie reviewed some photographs with Bobby. This time a quarter, not a trip to the fair, was used to encourage his participation. Bobby accurately identified pictures of several members of the Smith and Sager families. He identified those who were in the house and those who were not.

He became exasperated when Katie asked him if a photo showing a clean-shaven man wasn't the killer. "This is picture number five. This wasn't the man?"

Bobby shook his head. "Cause he ain't got a beard. Can't you see that? That's their dad," he stated correctly.

When shown comparison pictures of men with mustaches and beards, he agreed they looked like the man he had seen in the Smith house.

In 1986, when Bobby was 10, he again was interviewed by an NIS agent. With his more mature vocabulary, the boy was better equipped to describe what he had seen in August of 1981.

According to the investigator's report, Bobby's descriptions were "detailed and consistent with post-crime scene examination/interviews."

Bobby told the agent he remembered going to the Smiths' to spend the night. He recalled playing "cars" with the two youngest Sager children and sleeping on the floor with them. He said a "lady" also slept in the room, near the door.

He said the room was dark but the patio light provided some illumination. The boy remembered awakening and seeing a man "hit the lady" with a knife. The man then wiped the knife off on a cloth held in his other hand.

Bobby was terrified and tried to waken the child sleeping next to him by surreptitiously flicking him with his fingers. The man walked out the door to the hallway that leads to the stairs. Bobby heard the creaking of the stairs as someone walked up.

After the man left the room where the children and Sharon Sager's body were, the boy next to Bobby woke. Bobby whispered to him that someone was in the house but the groggy child went back to sleep.

Despite his terror, eventually Bobby's "eyelids got very tired" and he too went to sleep. He remembered nothing more until he was awakened by a military policeman the next morning.

The man Bobby saw kill Sharon Sager was shorter and stockier than Butch, according to Bobby's 1986 statement. The killer wore some type of ski-mask hat pulled down over the upper part of his face. He also wore a heavy jacket. He had a blond mustache and a sharp nose and carried a large-blade, survival-type knife and wore a knife pouch strapped around his leg.

Bobby speculated that the killer hadn't seen the three small boys curled up on sofa cushions in the corner. The corner was dark, he explained.

He may be right. Or, perhaps, Bobby was spared because whatever deranged rage directed the killer to slaughter Sharon Sager did not focus itself on small children. In any event, Bobby's instinct to be still and quiet saved his life. And perhaps, the lives of Scotty and Skippy.

Although physically uninjured, Bobby Davis was also one of the killer's victims, as was his family. For many years,

Bobby was unable to sleep in a room by himself. And, according to Sara Davis, the events of August 1981 contributed to the eventual break-up of her marriage.

Now, as then, she is convinced that Butch is innocent. "I heard he was watching scary movies that night and that's why he did it. That's ridiculous," she said.

"And a lot of people say he had a lot of emotional problems. There are a lot of people walking around in life with a lot of emotional problems. You just can't go by things like that. It could have been anybody. Why put it off on this child?"

CHAPTER 11

SECOND SUSPECT

Special Agent Michael Paul had been a policeman in St. Louis for 11 years before becoming an NIS agent. He had the macabre distinction of having examined more homicide crime scenes than any other Lejeune agent.

Former big-city policemen were generally respected but occasionally resented by fellow agents for their gritty wealth of experience.

Paul became case agent for the Kentucky Court slayings, responsible for reviewing witness statements and evidence reports. He was directly subordinate to Assistant Special Agent in Charge Mike Jones.

Paul later said that he thought many of the interviews were conducted haphazardly.

"It would go like this. The agent would say:

" 'Where were you that night?'

" 'I was home watching television.'

" 'Was anybody there?'

" 'Oh, no.'

"End of interview.

"That's bullshit. You go out and substantiate the alibi or tear it apart. If you can tear it apart, you've got a good lead."

From the start of the investigation, Paul had been skeptical that a 15-year-old, even one prone to violent temper tantrums, could have committed the carnage at Kentucky Court.

"The average person, who's probably never even hit anyone, doesn't know how to take someone out with a knife," Paul later said. "The person who killed these people knew exactly how to do it.

"When I ran it by Jones, 'how would Butch know how to kill these people,' his reply was, 'Well, you know, he reads *Soldier of Fortune* magazine.'

"*I* read *Soldier of Fortune* and half this base reads *Soldier of Fortune* and *I* didn't kill those people."

NIS had tunnel vision when it came to Butch, Paul later said, and it began the day the bodies were discovered.

The most plausible suspect to emerge that first day may have been Butch, but another person soon attracted Paul's attention, one he felt was a far more credible suspect.

While piecing together statements, Paul became suspicious of a witness whose alibi appeared to be shaky.

Navy Petty Officer William Kraagman,* 28, was a muscular man of middle height with a mustache that straggled over the edge of Navy regulations.

He was separated from his wife and, when he could afford it, lived alone.

Kraagman had met Betty several months before the slayings at the bar where she worked. A mutual acquaintance of several of Betty's friends, Kraagman had visited the Kentucky Court duplex more than once.

Several months after the murders, a female neighbor of the Smiths told Paul and Special Agent Peter Connolly that Connie confided in her a few weeks before the murders that Kraagman had tried to "play with her with his hands." Connie did not explain exactly what she meant, the woman said, but her impression was that Kraagman had tried to fondle her sexual organs.

He subsequently met Sharon at the bar. According to witnesses, Sharon had visited Kraagman at his apartment.

Kraagman told agents he gave Sharon amphetamines to help her stay alert during her drives to and from New York.

He also told agents Sharon had dropped by his apartment briefly while returning from Francis' trailer the day before the murders.

Kraagman was interviewed by NIS in September and would be interviewed again months later.

The night of the killings, Kraagman had been drinking heavily at a local bar, he told agents. During the evening he met two women and a male Marine who joined him at his table. The foursome had a couple of beers together before deciding to leave the bar.

They left the bar together and went to Kraagman's apartment where he picked up marijuana. They then drove to the women's trailer where Kraagman continued to drink beer and smoked the marijuana.

According to his companions' later statements to NIS agents, Kraagman also dropped LSD twice between midnight and 2:00 a.m.

He kept the drug – secreted in purple-colored micro dots – inside the cellophane wrapper of his cigarette pack.

Kraagman told Paul he left the women's trailer at 4:00 and returned to his apartment.

According to statements given by the Marine and two women, Kraagman was asked to leave after becoming verbally abusive and directing lewd remarks to both women.

"Let's go to the bedroom and screw around," he said to one of the women. When she declined, he turned to the other and said, "How about you?"

When the man told Kraagman to shut up, Kraagman began laughing and said, "What are you going to do, kick my ass?"

When the man angrily responded by taking off his shirt in preparation for a fight, Kraagman again laughed and walked out the door, slamming it behind him.

One of the women said she thought Kraagman had left the trailer between 2:30 and 3:00. The other said he left at about 4:30.

A witness, unconnected with the trailer incident, said Kraagman had confided in him that he had tried to have sex with Sharon Sager on two occasions. Kraagman said he had been unable to perform because of prior alcohol and drug use.

Kraagman's clinical record revealed a history of drunk driving arrests and treatment for alcoholism. More ominous, Kraagman had experienced repeated alcoholic blackouts, some lasting as long as 24 hours.

A former roommate said Kraagman often used alcohol, marijuana and amphetamines together.

"He was normally a quiet, subdued, shy individual," the former roommate told an agent. "However, on those frequent occasions when he took alcohol and drugs, his personality would change drastically. On those occasions, he would become loud, aggressive and actually violent, being on the verge of actively seeking physical confrontations with other individuals."

Other associates and co-workers of Kraagman's also noted he became belligerent when he drank.

When Kraagman again was interviewed by Paul and Connolly, Paul asked Kraagman, "Is it possible you killed those people during an alcoholic blackout?"

Kraagman slumped forward, dropped his head into his hands and said, "It's possible I had an alcoholic blackout that night. And, the bottom line is, if I did, I wouldn't know what I did."

The agents asked Kraagman if he was willing to take a polygraph. Kraagman agreed. Paul and Connolly hurriedly made arrangements for the test to be given the following morning.

"The next morning, Kraagman arrived at the NIS office and proceeded to tell me that not only was he not going to take the polygraph but he didn't want to talk to NIS anymore about the matter," Paul later recalled.

Paul wanted to begin an overt surveillance of Kraagman,

hoping to pressure him into incriminating acts or statements.

"I was told to back off and forget about it, drop the investigation of Kraagman," Paul said.

Paul was told by other agents that Kraagman's apartment had been searched shortly after the murders. Several knives and martial arts-type weapons were found, but none was seized.

The agent also was disturbed to find out that Kraagman's car had not been searched until more than a week after the killings. "Helen Keller would have had time to clean up that car after killing three people," Paul dryly remarked.

Later, Paul would not be able to find any report related to the search of Kraagman's home.

Several days after Kraagman was interrogated, an NIS secretary came into Paul's office.

"Somebody wants to talk about the homicides," she said. Paul recognized the young Marine who came into his office.

Cpl. Jerry Manfred* had been an NIS confidential source as part of a white-collar fraud investigation. He and Kraagman were occasional drinking buddies.

Kraagman had stopped by Manfred's quarters the day before, Manfred said, and had become increasingly agitated and despondent. Suddenly, he looked down at his hands and said, "You know, NIS could be right. I may have killed those people."

Manfred added that Kraagman habitually kept a particular knife by his bed. The day after the killings, Manfred had noticed that the knife had been replaced with another.

Paul told Manfred not to reveal to Kraagman that he had spoken to him. Manfred was told to watch Kraagman and report what he observed.

Paul later testified in court that, while looking through NIS files, he had been unable to find the sworn statement and formal notes he turned in concerning the initial meeting with Manfred. They were important, Paul said, because they established that Manfred was more than a casual witness. He was actually working in cooperation with NIS during the investigation.

"I gave it a good diligent search and was unable to find that information," Paul testified.

Although he got nothing more of significance from Manfred, Paul did get additional information about Kraagman from others.

A lance corporal who worked with Kraagman said he told him much the same thing he had told the two NIS agents the year before, that he could have experienced an alcoholic black-out at the time of the homicides. He added that not long after the murders, Kraagman claimed to have driven to Virginia in an alcoholic blackout.

A former acquaintance told Paul that Kraagman had such a morbid fascination with his own checkered past that he kept an album of all his arrests, including DUIs and assaults.

"Anything he got in trouble with that was in the paper was in his album. I mean. it wasn't a little-bitty book. It was a BOOK! Which I thought rather strange. I mean, those kind of things you don't like to be reminded of."

A woman who dated Kraagman after the homicides said he had tried to engage in sexual intercourse with her on several occasions but was unable to perform.

She added that she and Kraagman once had been in the bar where Betty worked. Kraagman, eyeing Betty, told her he really wanted to have sex with Betty.

She was offended that Kraagman, who'd been unable to have sex with her, was fantasizing about Betty.

One of Kraagman's friends told Paul that shortly after the killings, Kraagman was driving him to an auto repair shop when the conversation turned to the homicides and, especially, the fact that one of the victims had been a little girl.

Kraagman began to weep uncontrollably and strike his fists against the dashboard of the car, the friend told Paul. He sobbed, "If I ever find out who did it, I'll take care of them myself."

His friend was so alarmed that he pulled the car off the road so Kraagman could walk around and regain his compo-sure.

Much later, Betty's friend and former neighbor Susan

Rodriguez would remember seeing Kraagman and two other men in the diner where she worked as a waitress. She would recall the men talking heatedly about the murders and Kraagman "boasting about blood squirting all over the walls."

Kraagman's prints were sent to the FBI for comparison with prints taken at the crime scene. In the summer of 1982, the FBI reported that additional impressions were needed to eliminate Kraagman conclusively as the source of the bloody palm print found on the sliding glass door next to Sharon Sager's body.

Were more of Kraagman's prints sent to the FBI? Case records given to prosecutors by NIS do not report any such follow-up. Paul knew why there was no follow-up on Kraagman. His superiors at NIS were convinced that they already knew who had committed the murders: Butch Smith.

CHAPTER 12

SECOND GO-ROUND

Butch was officially interviewed again on September 26, this time less cordially than before.

The interview was held at the Holiday Inn in Jacksonville instead of NIS headquarters. Betty and Gary Francis waited in a separate room with a connecting door left open. They were unable to hear the conversation.

The interview lasted about three hours, without any breaks, and it was not taped. NIS Special Agents Mike Jones, Deborah Cobb and Gordon Crossman were the interrogators.

Butch was told that he was a suspect and advised of his rights. When Jones asked if he understood his rights and wanted a lawyer, Butch asked why he was a suspect. The agents' reports would not say what explanation he was given.

According to Butch, it was during this interview that he learned for the first time what agents believed was his motive. He was alleged to have been involved in an incestuous relationship with Connie. Fear that his mother would discover the relationship was allegedly Butch's motive for the killings.

Jones' report does state that during the explanation of why he was a suspect, Butch became agitated, pounding his fists on the wall and hurling an ashtray across the room.

Butch soon cooled down. He signed the waiver of his rights, telling Jones he did not want a lawyer nor desire to keep silent.

Asked to write his thoughts on the murders, Butch wrote that he thought someone who'd followed the family back from New York had done it.

Butch's written remarks, as well as the statement he signed, later would be misplaced.

During the interview, Butch described dreams he'd had about the murders.

In one recurring dream, his aunt, cousin and sister stood over his bed. They tried to tell him who killed them by flashing a picture of the murderer on the wall. Butch was unable to identify the person in the picture and he could not hear what the victims were saying.

As discussion of the murders continued, Butch speculated that his aunt and cousin were killed while lying on their backs. A knife was thrust in their throats and slashed downward, he said.

He said Connie was killed when she unexpectedly came in the house and discovered the killer. He said he thought the killer grabbed Connie around the neck, covered her mouth with his gloved right hand and stabbed her with the knife in his left hand.

He said the killer stabbed his sister in the chest and sliced with a "downward motion." Then, he said, the killer put her on the sofa in the living room.

Butch's mentioning the glove and Connie's abdominal wound would become highly significant. Agents would contend his awareness of her wound and the possibility that the killer wore a glove showed guilty knowledge.

But by this time Butch had heard interminable discussions of the murders. It would be unusual if someone had not concluded there were no incriminating bloody fingerprints found at the scene. Otherwise, why hadn't the agents arrested anyone?

It would logically follow that someone would guess there was a dearth of prints because the killer wore gloves.

To wear only one glove, of course, would defeat the purpose. Even if the killer wielded the knife with one hand, both his hands would inevitably be stained with blood.

Connie's wound was the topic of wide-spread discussion. As early as August 28, *The Daily News* in Jacksonville reported witnesses saw Connie Smith with her throat slashed and a "long, deep laceration extending from the top of her forehead to her lower abdomen, according to one source."

Long before Butch's interview on September 26, newspaper accounts were describing Connie's body as "disemboweled."

The direction of Connie's post mortem wound was from the genitals up to the chest, not "downward." And she was killed as she lay on the couch, probably while asleep.

If Butch were guilty, he either was intentionally misleading agents or had a poor memory of the killings.

During the same interview, Butch said he thought that the killer had a mustache and resembled Burt Reynolds. He said the man was about five-feet, nine-inches tall, wore a dark blue T-shirt covered with blood, wore a glove on his right hand and used a military bayonet as the weapon.

Butch volunteered the information that he had twice visited his sister's and cousin's graves while in New York for the funerals. He said he told the deceased he was sorry. When asked to explain, Butch said he was sorry they were killed.

The agents were already aware of what Butch had said at the grave sites because he had been videotaped.

Butch was asked what punishment he thought the killer deserved. He said the killer should be sent to prison unless he's a "psycho," in which case he should get help.

He said he enjoyed reading *Soldier of Fortune* magazine but denied ever discussing a 1980 article called "Silent Death" with anyone.

The question about *Soldier of Fortune* resulted from an NIS interview with a Navy corpsman earlier that September. The corpsman and his wife had briefly stayed in the Smith's quarters when they arrived at Camp Lejeune in 1980. At the time, Betty's husband had already left for Okinawa.

The corpsman told an NIS agent that during the visit, Butch had asked him about an article in *Soldier of Fortune.*

"Butch questioned me about an article in *Soldier of Fortune* magazine depicting a knife technique which involved placing a hand over the mouth of the victim from behind, placing a knee in the small of the back and, with a slashing motion, cutting the victim's throat," the statement said.

"This technique is designed to kill the victim quietly. Therefore, it's called 'the silent death,' " the corpsman said. He added that the article appeared in 1980.

There was a 1978 *Soldier of Fortune* article titled "Silent Death." But the article concerned Special Forces snipers in Vietnam. It had nothing to do with knives.

The article the corpsman referred to may have been one titled "Sentry Removal." It depicts a ninja-type knife attack on an unsuspecting sentry. The attack requires the assassin to jump on the victim's back. The assassin then wraps his legs around the victim's torso to immobilize his arms.

The technique apparently requires an assassin with gymnastics skills and a victim able – and willing – to remain standing with arms at his sides while a ninja leaps on his back.

This article appeared in 1978. If Butch saved back-issues, he didn't keep them at home. There were no *Soldier of Fortune* magazines seized from the Smith quarters.

Interestingly, in several respects, including the mustache and the color of the killer's shirt, Butch's conjectural description of the killer resembled that given by another witness. Whether Butch had gleaned this description from conversations with other children is unclear.

At one point in the interview, Butch glared at Crossman. "At that time, Mr. Smith looked me in the face," Crossman wrote in his report. "He said, 'You think I killed them, don't you?' I said, 'Yes, I do. The evidence points to that.' "

When told the agents believed the killer was someone familiar with the residence and its occupants, Butch stalked angrily from the room.

Francis later testified to the interview's abrupt end: "That interview concluded with Butch storming out of the adjacent room, through the room that we were occupying, out the front door of the room we were in, and down the veranda of the hotel, with me quickly behind him to find out what was going on and to settle him down because I didn't know what he was going to do, if he was going to throw himself off the veranda, or what.

"I approached him and tried to ascertain what took place. He indicated to me that they had told him that they believed he was guilty.

"I indicated to him that as far as he was concerned, if he wanted it to be, the interview was over. We could get in the car and go home," Francis said. And that was what they did.

Francis suggested that Betty get advice from the local lawyer who was handling Francis' divorce. The lawyer told Betty to refuse to allow agents to interview Butch further. She followed his advice.

CHAPTER 13

DOUBTS AND PSYCHIATRISTS

After the Sager children and Debbie Dash had been reclaimed by their respective fathers, Betty, Butch and Lorrie had moved into the trailer where Gary Francis had lived. He and his roommate returned to the barracks.

Soon afterward, Lorrie went to Florida to visit her natural father and his wife. Lorrie did not want to return to Camp Lejeune. She told an investigator she wished to move because she feared her brother.

But she later said that hadn't been true, that she'd simply been desperate to get away from Camp Lejeune. Butch had just been the most credible excuse, she said.

During the weeks after the murders, Butch would sometimes ride his bike to Tom Cheek's house, much to the neighbors' dismay.

"From what I understand," Tom later recalled, "some people actually called the MPs and complained about him being out there. But he had every right to be there because he was our guest."

After the complaints, however, the boys usually visited at Francis' trailer.

The trailer park bordered a Marine training area that was officially off-limits but was an irresistible lure to the boys. Butch and Tom liked to scavenge the area for items abandoned after training exercises.

"We'd gather up the rations, and what was good we'd keep," Tom said. "They left live M-16 rounds out there. We'd pick all that up too. "Once, we walked into what we thought was an empty tent. There was a Marine in there, getting ready for an exercise."

The boys hastily departed, the startled Marine angrily shouting behind them.

The Christmas after the killings, Tom and a friend who was visiting from Cherry Point went to the trailer to visit Butch.

"We were drinking eggnog and got pretty smashed and silly," Tom recalled. The boys were mocking each other with outrageous threats. Tom's friend joked that they were going to cut off Butch's "privates" and then everyone would call him "Stumpy."

"Butch laughed so hard he knocked the Christmas tree over," Tom said.

It was during the time he was staying at Gary Francis' trailer, Butch later recalled, that he tried cocaine. One afternoon he had decided not to go to the beach with Betty and Francis, but had tooled around on his bike. He stopped at the trailer belonging to a Marine who had befriended the boy after the crimes. When Butch stuck his head in the unlocked door, he saw the man was preparing a line of cocaine.

Butch recognized the drug and asked if he might try some. The man reacted in surprise, then agreed.

Butch said he thought the man allowed him to use the drug because he figured Butch would be less likely to tell what he had seen.

Butch said he was not pleased with the drug's effect and did not use it again.

By this time, Butch had begun the school year at Lejeune High School, not far from Kentucky Court. The school's enrollment is limited to students whose parents live on base. For the most part, he said, the kids left him alone but he often felt they were talking behind his back.

While at school, he was under overt surveillance by NIS agents, a situation many of the students probably knew about.

Former Special Agent Paul later testified: "Myself and a number of other agents were directed to sit outside the high school and wait until Butch came out and got on the bus. We followed the bus home every day. It was a daily occurrence.

"The idea was to let Butch know we were looking at him as a suspect and, second of all, to see if we could get a reaction of some kind."

After Butch's second interview with NIS agents, his mother indicated that even she had doubts about his innocence.

Her friend and former neighbor, Susan Rodriguez, told an NIS agent that Betty visited her home in late September and told her that NIS believed Butch committed the murders. When she asked Betty who she thought had done it, Rodriguez said, Betty said she was afraid that it had been Butch.

"But they'll never get Butch. I know him better than anyone," Rodriguez said Betty quickly added.

Several weeks later, Betty again spoke with Rodriguez, who reported the conversations to the same NIS agent. She said Betty told her she planned to go into hiding with Butch until the homicide investigation had "blown over." Betty said NIS had told her they had some new evidence that implicated Butch, who was acting increasingly troubled.

In early October, NIS asked a psychiatrist at the Naval Regional Medical Center at Camp Lejeune to compile a psychological profile of Butch, using the results of previous examinations and interviews with counselors. Butch himself was not examined.

The doctor noted the limitations of making a diagnosis from documents without actually talking to the patient.

"It is appreciated that this entire psychiatric profile was compiled through a review of the references listed above.

While the validity of such information is always questionable, much observational consistency was noted with regard to many behavioral characteristics."

Despite the pitfalls of a "paper" diagnosis, the doctor said of Butch, "numerous traits consistent with a sociopathic personality organization are present."

This diagnosis was a step-up in gravity from the "adjustment reaction of adolescence" diagnosis reached by the Eckerd camp consulting psychiatrist.

The profile was forwarded to Duke University Medical Center, where Butch was sent for psychiatric evaluation on November 3. He stayed until December 18. The evaluation was requested by NIS in case Butch was indicted for the murders. If so, it would be necessary to determine if he were mentally competent to stand trial.

When he arrived at the prestigious hospital, he had a cold. His weight had dropped to 139 pounds. Butch did not find his hospitalization unpleasant, although he disliked one doctor.

"He'd ask questions that no matter how you answered, you looked guilty," Butch complained. "Like, how do you suppose it happened?"

Doctors and staff were aware that Butch was the prime suspect in a triple homicide.

"Initially, everyone was frightened until they got to know Butch, who was well-liked by the staff and his peers on the ward," said the doctor's final report. "He caused no further fear or distrust among the patients or staff. He participated in ward activities and worked in psychotherapy. He was also sent to adolescent group."

Results of a myriad of tests suggested "long-standing learning difficulties despite average intelligence."

Butch told one of the psychiatrists that math was his most troublesome subject in school. He remarked on math's irrelevance for one who plans to "go into the Marines and shoot the enemy."

The diagnosis was: "Conduct disorder, socialized, aggressive; and mixed personality disorder with hysterical and impulse control features."

"Personality testing suggests an impulse control disorder with a tendency to act out if provoked," reported one psychiatrist. "Butch's strengths include his outgoing, non-isolated way of relating, and his awareness of his own needs for affection and support."

One of the Duke psychiatrists subsequently wrote a letter stating that he had determined, in response to government inquiry, that Butch was not mentally ill at the time of the killings. And, if Butch did commit the killings, he knew right from wrong.

In the letter, the psychiatrist expressed concern for his former patient and said he hoped every effort would be made to see that Butch continued to have treatment. He seemed to have some reservations about whether those efforts would be made.

"It concerns me that I have not been allowed to provide Dr. Mark Gillam* the information we have accumulated to help with on-going treatment. ... As I have not had any follow-up from Dr. Gillam, it is impossible for me to know how things are going at this time."

But to base officials, Butch's primary status was no longer that of a military dependent in need of medical treatment. It was that of prime suspect in a murder investigation.

Susan Rodriguez called NIS again in December and said that Betty had told her Butch was much improved since his stay at Duke. She said Betty also told her that her relationship with Gary Francis was troubled.

CHAPTER 14

MORE SUSPECTS

Betty Smith insisted that she cooperated with agents until they began to use what she viewed as stormtrooper tactics on Butch. She said that immediately after the murders, before she knew Butch was a suspect, she offered to allow him and Lorrie to be questioned under hypnosis as Chris Sager had been. But agents never arranged such an interview.

Betty felt that NIS had treated her as though she herself were a criminal.

It was true that some agents harbored a scarcely concealed contempt for Betty because of her relationship with Francis. An officer involved in the investigation said Puritanical attitudes – and hypocrisy – were not uncommon at Camp Lejeune.

"That kind of infidelity, the woman having an affair while the man is away defending the country, is scorned. Notwithstanding what the deployed hero might be doing in the Philippines."

Betty and Francis were equally unhappy with NIS. In early January of 1982, Betty asked Michael Paul to meet the couple in the parking lot of the naval hospital.

Betty felt Paul was more sympathetic to the family's situation and less convinced of Butch's guilt than other agents. While keeping surveillance on the family, Paul had occasionally stopped by the trailer where Betty and Butch were living. Betty felt he had listened objectively to her complaints about NIS treatment of Butch.

She told Paul that at one point Butch had been about to confess to the crimes because of the enormous pressure placed upon him by NIS. She said she and Francis had talked Butch out of it.

Betty proffered the names of two people that she and Francis felt were likely suspects. Sleeper and Jones, she said, had never seriously considered any suspects other than Butch.

Sleeper and Jones had identified Butch as the prime suspect, but agents had considered others as well. Betty was unaware that Kraagman was being investigated. And later there could be no question that another suspect of whom she also was unaware was capable of murder.

A former Marine private named Bailey*, who had been on unauthorized absence from Camp Lejeune at the time of the killings, was convicted of killing a woman in New Jersey in 1982.

Bailey and another man had picked up a female hitchhiker. While the other man was driving, Bailey had stabbed the woman to death with a knife. The knife Bailey used was double-edged and had a leather pouch.

He was sentenced to life in prison.

A fellow inmate later said he overheard Bailey say, "They got me for her, but there are two they'll never get me for."

A check of Bailey's previous whereabouts revealed he had been stationed at Camp Lejeune in 1981, and a prison psychologist said, given the right circumstances, Bailey could have committed the Lejeune murders.

Bailey openly admitted a hatred for women but denied to the psychologist that he had committed any murder other than the one for which he was convicted. He also denied committing the burglaries for which he was convicted.

Bailey told the psychologist that before he was imprisoned he would work during the day and be "intact" but at night would find himself "on the prowl."

He was dropped as a suspect in the Camp Lejeune murders after the FBI determined that the bloody fingerprint found on the toybox in the playroom where Sharon Sager died was not his.

Because Bailey had a broken finger and eczema on both hands at the time the prints were taken, they could not be used for comparison with other unidentified prints found at the murder scene.

Another lead was a man nicknamed "Whip." He was a regular at the bar where Betty worked. An off-duty policeman who was in the bar August 26 noticed Whip resembled a composite drawing of the murder suspect that was circulating among law enforcement officers.

The policeman struck up a conversation with Whip, who had four parallel scratches on the right side of his neck, extending from below his ear to his collarbone.

Whip told the policeman he'd been working at the construction site of the new naval hospital as well as working at odd jobs off-base. The hospital site is less than two miles from Watkins Village.

The two briefly discussed the murders, which Whip said he knew little about. Talk then turned to deer hunting and Whip told the policeman he usually gutted deer from the neck down rather than from the genitals to the neck, which is how most hunters do it.

Whip showed the policeman the knife he carried strapped to his leg and mentioned other knives he had at home.

He told the policeman he had a lot of problems at home and was interested in "getting the bartender," who was a woman.

"At one point he pulled out his knife and opened it up and told me that if she bent over the bar again he would 'cut off her tits' and take them home with him," the policeman said.

During their conversation, Whip also said that he was a former Marine and sometimes sold dope on base.

The policeman recounted the episode to an NIS agent three days later.

When agents questioned Whip, he said he did not recall the conversation with the policeman and had only been at Camp Lejeune twice. He did say his girlfriend's brother was dating "one of the Smith girls" but he did not know the first name. The agents decided it was improbable that he had anything to do with the crimes.

Another possibility that agents had considered and dismissed was that a stranger was responsible for the murders.

"Would a pervert in the neighborhood who'd been watching be inclined to walk in that house not knowing what he'd run into?" one agent asked.

"Someone would have had to have surveilled the house for some time, seen Mrs. Smith drive off and known she hadn't returned with her boyfriend."

But Betty and Gary, talking with Paul in the hospital parking lot, were unaware that anyone but Butch was being investigated.

After expressing her frustration with NIS, Betty told Paul that she wanted very much to leave the Jacksonville area. But she was financially unable, she said, because all her possessions were still locked up at Kentucky Court.

But under no circumstances would she leave, she said, unless Gary Francis was transferred where they could be together.

CHAPTER 15

LAB RESULTS

By late January 1982, NIS had gotten back evidence submitted to the FBI. The lab had discovered a latent print, either palm or finger, on the knife stained with Connie's blood that was found in Tyler's bed. But the print did not match those of anybody known to be in the apartment on the night of the murders.

If the print did not come from Butch, the victims or any of the surviving children, where did it come from?

The knife already had been examined by SBI Special Agent Stephen R. Jones on August 27. At that time, Jones reported that no latent prints were noted. Either he failed to find the print or it was somehow put on the knife between August and January.

Jones later would concede that the FBI, having access to extremely sophisticated testing facilities, may have found something he overlooked.

"They were working in a laboratory situation and I was working at the crime scene," he explained.

He had been unaware NIS planned to send the knife to the FBI for further processing. And he doubted the FBI was aware the knife had been previously processed.

"They probably took it at face value that it had not been. If they were going to send it to the FBI, then I should never have touched it."

The print, Jones conceded, may have been his.

"After I finished processing it, I might have handled it, putting it in a package," he said of the knife. "I'm not saying it's my palm print. But I'm not saying it couldn't be either."

The print on the knife was just one piece of evidence examined by either the SBI or FBI that pointed to someone other than Butch as the killer.

A quarter-size bloodstain found on a T-shirt in the upstairs hallway was discovered not to have come from Butch or any of the victims.

The FBI also determined that a bloody palm print found on the sliding glass door beside Sharon Sager's body was not Butch's or that of any other member of the household.

One agent suggested that a medical technician may have left the print. But the print's location, inside the drapery, indicated someone intentionally parted the curtain and tried to open the door. An accidental lunge against the door would have left blood on both the drapery and the glass.

Other evidence also pointed away from Butch. Two reddish-brown beard hairs, one cut and one "forcibly removed," were discovered on a towel. A forcibly-removed hair has been pulled out of the follicle, either with an implement – such as tweezers – or by hand.

The towel, found thrown on the back of the couch where Sharon Sager's body lay, also contained scalp hairs from each of the three victims.

The beard hairs did not match hair samples from Butch or the other boys in the apartment, none of whom had begun to shave.

Had the killer wiped these beard hairs off, as well as the

victims' hair and blood, while cleaning up? If so, it would indicate that he returned to the playroom after killing the two children.

Had the forcibly-removed hair been plucked during a victim's defensive struggle?

Despite the presence of physical evidence that pointed away from Butch and the lack of any connecting him to the killings, NIS continued its tunnel vision of Butch as the murderer.

Later, one agent would offer a curiously convoluted explanation for this: There must have been evidence showing Butch did it because Butch did do it, the agent said. But because the crime scene was a "zoo," the evidence that would have proved Butch's guilt was accidentally destroyed or overlooked.

"I don't understand what's not there," Mike Duncan said. "That's what frustrates a cop. You think and you think and you can't account for something and it starts to eat at you."

Without question the investigation was flawed, some agents later acknowledged, but agents on military reservations work in an extraordinary situation.

"There are too many people that control," one agent said. "Too many people that can shut it down, say, no, you're not talking to this person. Too many people that can control the cop.

"In the civilian police, the district attorney can prevent too much interference. In the end, the mayor's got to answer to the voters. A general isn't elected."

Agents on a military base also are subject to special protocol, another agent said.

"On a military installation, you've got a general and chief of staff that want to come over. How can you say no?"

By January, Betty had rented her own trailer off-base. School officials told Betty that Butch was no longer eligible to attend Lejeune High School. Betty enrolled him in the high school in the small waterfront town of Swansboro.

Butch later said that he "caught hell" there.

Other students left notes, drawings and newspaper clippings in his locker. His only happy memory of the school would be a brief stint on the baseball team. He played in one game.

During this time, Butch spent some time with his dad but saw little of Gary Francis.

"He was more interested in Mama than anything," Butch said of Francis.

Betty was miserable in North Carolina. When Francis was sent to Okinawa that spring, she decided to move to her parents' home in New York despite NIS's request that she and Butch not leave the area.

"I called from New York," Betty said, "and told them where they could find me."

Butch enrolled in high school in Springville, but many of the students were aware that he was a suspect in a murder case and he became as unhappy as he had been in Swansboro.

By May, he had already been in a fight with a student who taunted him about the murders. Betty said that Butch was pushed to the ground and struck his head hard enough to warrant medical attention.

An NIS agent later interviewed students at the school. A 16-year-old girl, who had ridden the same bus as Butch, told the agent Butch once said he wanted to go in the Army so he could kill people. The girl said another student told Butch, "You can't just go around killing people." According to the girl, Butch replied that he had killed before and he would kill again.

She also told the agent that Butch said he had raped his old girlfriend.

Betty was asked to withdraw Butch from the school.

It was about this time that Butch again began to have recurring nightmares about the murders and a haze-obscured killer. Betty told Michael Paul that she had taken Butch to a psychologist. During the last session, Betty said, she suggested that Butch undergo hypnosis to see if he could recall the killer's face.

Butch interjected that he was no longer having the nightmares. The psychologist said, in that case, it might be unwise to make Butch remember the incident.

In the summer of 1981, Marine Capt. F. Reid Bogie had been the only special assistant at the Camp Lejeune base legal office. The mission of the special assistant is to prosecute civilians who commit crimes on military bases. Although they are military officers, usually holding the rank of captain or major, special assistants appearing in federal court often choose not to wear their uniforms in order to appear "more homogenous."

When Capt. Bogie had returned from a family trip to Connecticut a week after the murders, he had been assigned the job of regularly evaluating NIS reports and weighing the merits of evidence.

"When something new came in, we'd ask, how does this fit in to what we already know?"

Bogie would then brief the staff judge advocate, a colonel. "I had to tell him what I thought and why. More than once, I had to defend my position," Bogie said. The colonel and Capt. Bogie were well aware of how urgently base officials desired an arrest.

At one point, Bogie later said, Butch and Kraagman both had merited – and gotten – intense scrutiny.

"I always thought they were equally credible. But Butch had the edge because he was definitely there."

By the summer of 1982, however, Bogie had determined that there was not enough evidence to indict Butch.

"All the evidence came within three inches of Butch, then – boom – there was nothing," Bogie said. "I couldn't, in good conscience, indict Butch. Notwithstanding the fact that I suspect, even now, that he did it."

The decision not to indict was based on evidence. But there were other peculiarities of the case that stymied a whole-hearted conviction on Bogie's part that Butch was the killer.

"One of the things that was hard to overcome in this is that it's very difficult to conceptualize a 15-year-old doing something like this."

Bogie cited Connie's post-mortem wounds, which he described as "demonic."

"I was also struck by how clean Butch was. Here's this crime so vicious that there's blood on the ceiling but this 15-year-old, who's supposed to have done it, has no blood on him."

Francis had returned from Okinawa on a hardship transfer to take custody of his three children in Colorado Springs. Betty and Butch joined him there during the summer of 1982.

"I couldn't let Mom drive all that way alone," Butch explained.

Francis and Betty were married September 13, 1982 – Friday the 13th.

Friction between Butch and Francis began almost immediately. Butch said he resented not being allowed to discuss his dad or call him from the Francis home.

"I'd call him from a pay phone at school," Butch said.

Lorrie was still living with her natural father in Florida.

Michael Paul called Francis in October of 1982, before the family reported to Camp Pendleton, Calif.

Francis told Paul he was aware agents had been questioning students and staff at Butch's former school in Springville. He said he hoped the move to Pendleton would put an end to the investigation. Francis said he especially hoped it would put an end to what Francis viewed as Mike Jones' harassment of Butch.

Francis said he wanted to move his family into on-base housing at Camp Pendleton but expected base housing officials would deny his request at the suggestion of NIS. He told Paul he planned to get out of the Marines when his enlistment was up and try to get a job as a police officer.

In California, Butch started his junior year at Fallbrook High School where many students were dependents of Marines stationed at Camp Pendleton.

"It was a piece of cake, only two required courses," Butch recalled.

Francis got out of the Marine Corps in August of 1983 and moved the family to Lyons, Ore., a rural community about 80 miles from Vale.

Lorrie was again living with her mother and Francis. Her boyfriend was a dairyman's son. She earned money helping with the morning milking.

When the dairyman was short-handed, Lorrie asked Butch if he'd like to help at the farm, and he said yes. He was hired and also helped the dairyman lay the foundation for a new barn.

"I didn't relish getting up at 4:00 a.m. but I always had a little money to spend," Butch recalled of his job. He was grateful for the dairy farmer's kindness to him and Lorrie. "But I've hated cows ever since," Butch wryly recalled. After a few weeks, the farmer was no longer able to pay Butch but he continued to help out at the farm anyway.

Butch did not return to school for his senior year, a decision he blamed on the unhappy situation at home. Instead, he joined the Job Corps and studied heavy equipment operation at Fort Simcoe, Ore., for 18 months. In exchange for training and a $50 a week wage, Job Corps workers made highway repairs and improvements in national parks. It was one of the happiest periods of Butch's life. He went home every other weekend.

After finishing the Job Corps program, he worked sporadically operating a bulldozer for a construction company. Occasionally, he lived in a trailer on his employer's property.

At the time, the Francis family was living in a somewhat isolated area, "like 'Little House on the Prairie'," according to Betty. Because Butch did not have a driver's license, it was difficult for him to find work.

He had earned a General Equivalency Diploma to compensate for not finishing high school, but it seemed to have little effect on his ability to get a job. He had tried to join the Navy but had not scored quite high enough on the entrance examination. With what he saw as very few options, Butch made a momentous decision. He would join the National Guard.

Lorrie, Connie, Butch and their mother Betty
Smith, Christmas, 1979. Butch was on a "home
visit" from Eckerd wilderness camp.

Photo taken in New York, shortly before the family returned to Camp Lejeune in August, 1981.
From left to right on coach are: Debbie, Connie,
unidentified cousin, Butch and Tyler. Seated on
floor, from left, are: Tommy, Skippy, Scotty,
Chris and Lorrie.

Butch Smith is photographed at NIS headquarters the day of the killings. NIS suspected one of the victims scratched Butch. But Tommy said Chris cut Butch's cheek by accident while Butch was working on a model. Butch said he cut his wrist compressing the garbage.

The ambulance pulled up to the front door of the Smith residence. The duplex at left was unoccupied the night of the murders. Top of station wagon where Debbie and Lorrie slept is visible next to the covered walkway on right side of building. The first-floor window at right is room where Connie was killed. Second floor window at right is room where Chris slept. Narrow unobscured window above walkway is room where Tyler died. NIS field operations center was set up in the tent at left. Photo by Randy Davey, used by permission of *The Daily News*, Jacksonville, N.C.

NIS agents gather at field operations center set up on Kentucky Court August 24, 1981. Photo by Randy Davey, used by permission of *The Daily News*, Jacksonville, N.C.

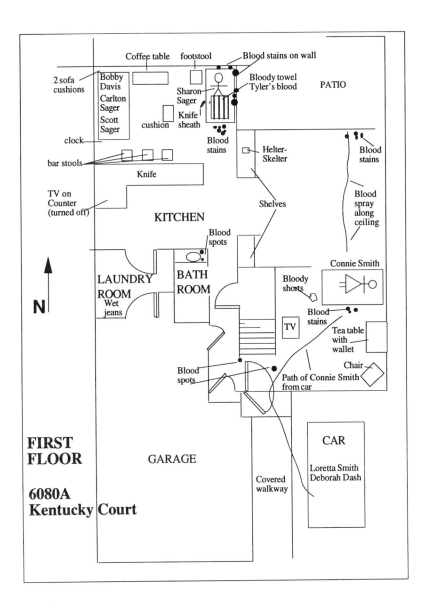

Floor plan of first floor of Smith residence, showing location of blood stains, bodies, furniture and other information

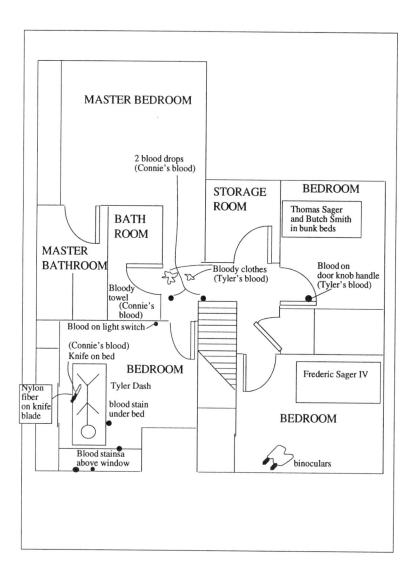

Floor plan of second floor of Smith residence, showing location of blood stains, bodies, furniture and other information

Butch is led from courtroom by sheriff's deputies after first appearance in Onslow County District Court, December 14, 1988. Photo by Randy Davey.

Attorney Chuck Henry, left, confers with Butch in Onslow County Superior Court in February, 1989. Photo by Don Bryan, used with permission of *The Daily News*, Jacksonville, N.C.

CHAPTER 16

CASE REOPENED

By 1986, the investigation had lain fallow for five years. Two events would revitalize it: Butch Smith's effort to join the Oregon Army National Guard and a Marine captain's decision to – at last – prosecute.

Capt. Matthew Bogdanos was one of those splendid few Marine lawyers selected to serve as special assistants to the U.S. attorney. In 1986, Bogdanos took the job at Camp Lejeune that R. Reid Bogie had filled in 1981.

Bogdanos' boss, the staff judge advocate, was Col. Richard A. Vogel. Brash and engaging, Bogdanos was a native of New York City and a Columbia Law School graduate. His polished patter came naturally.

Of the many case files Bogdanos reviewed while familiarizing himself with his new job, one was striking. An unsolved triple homicide dating back to 1981. The Butch Smith case.

"It was an enormous press case," Bogdanos recalled. "This

was the number one case." But by 1986, he explained, it was no longer a priority because "people believed all leads had been exhausted."

Bogdanos knew the lack of evidence was a problem.

"Those in charge before me, based on their judgment – which was sound judgment – believed there was not enough evidence to warrant trying him. No one prior to me would authorize an arrest," he recalled.

"I saw a couple of things I thought should be done, evidence I thought had more value than my predecessors thought."

At about this same time, another man also was reviewing the Smith case. NIS Special Agent Stephen Freeman, described by Bogdanos as a "super agent," took over the Crimes of Violence Squad at Camp Lejeune in 1986.

Freeman approached the base legal office for advice. He was concerned about whether the lapse of time would pose legal problems if the Butch Smith case were reopened.

Freeman was reassured that should he find sufficient evidence, a warrant could be issued.

A law enforcement officer may get an arrest warrant on the basis of physical evidence, eyewitness testimony or confession. There was no physical evidence to implicate Butch. The testimony of the sole eyewitness exonerated him. That left the possibility of arresting Butch on the basis of a confession.

Freeman decided NIS would interview Butch again. The plan was to locate Butch through routine procedures such as driver's license registration.

But this proved unnecessary when Staff Sgt. Kevin McMorris called from Oregon requesting Butch's medical records.

What McMorris learned from Butch's records – that the young man had an ominously unhealthy psychological profile and had made inconsistent statements to investigators about the murders – led, of course, to Butch being rejected by the National Guard.

Betty Smith Francis was outraged. Again, the family seemed unable to escape the events of August, 1981.

She made several angry calls to NIS. In one of her calls, she threatened to seek a congressional inquiry if the investigation were not resolved.

Her frustration sprang from more than motherly concern. Butch had been sporadically employed as a construction worker but was having difficulty finding permanent full-time work.

Gary Francis was not pleased that his 20-year-old stepson was again living with him and Betty.

There had been several rows. At least one of the rows, according to Lorrie Smith, who also was living with Francis and her mother, ended with Francis and Butch in an altercation.

There had been alternating war and truce between Butch and his second stepfather from the beginning.

"I liked him OK," Butch later said. "But he wasn't my dad."

Francis described his relationship with Butch as "tumultuous."

Francis had been in the process of divorcing his first wife when he met Betty. His tour of duty in Okinawa, which began in March of 1982, was cut short six months later when his ex-wife relinquished custody of their three children to him.

Even under the best of circumstances, a combined family poses serious adjustment problems. Conflicts between stepfathers and adolescent sons are common. The additional stress of Butch's emotional problems, the trauma of the unresolved killings at Lejeune and the relocations and separations required of service members brought perilous pressure on Francis' marriage to Betty.

Francis was a rugged military policeman, a former Air Force drill instructor and Marine brig security guard. According to Betty, he felt his authority over his wife and children was near absolute.

"He even told me who I was to vote for," Betty recalled. But even after their marriage ended, Betty tried to be scrupulously fair when describing the relationship between Francis and Butch.

When asked who provoked the disagreements between

stepfather and stepson, Betty said, "I'd say it was 50-50."

By 1986, Francis was working as a weighmaster for the state of Oregon. But he wanted to return to law enforcement with the Gresham Police Department. He was concerned that Butch's background was hampering his chances for a job as a civilian policeman.

"They didn't want him to move to Gresham and bring Butch," Betty later said.

When the murder investigation followed the family to Oregon and Butch was denied enlistment in the National Guard, the emotional punch threw them up against the ropes for the last time.

Betty immediately called Camp Lejeune and spoke to Special Agent Stephen Freeman.

"She was extremely upset," Freeman was later to say. "She felt that the Naval Investigative Service had deliberately prevented him from enlisting in the National Guard and that we were harassing the family after all these years."

Freeman was able to calm her. He assured her that he, as much as she, wished to see the matter resolved. A resolution, however, would mean allowing agents to interview Butch again.

Several days later, according to Freeman, Betty called him back and said the family was willing to be interviewed.

Freeman and CID Agent John Rodgers flew to Oregon and spoke to McMorris as well as Butch's previous employers. They took Gary, Betty and Butch to dinner.

"He came across as a really nice guy, full of feeling," Betty later said of Freeman. "He was going to help Butch out."

Butch also thought the agents were sympathetic, and wanted to help him prove his innocence.

The atmosphere was restrained, according to Francis.

"They wanted to interview Butch and, if things checked out – if things felt the right way, then, to put it in Agent Freeman's words, 'Slam dunk, we're out of here.' "

The Francises agreed to arrange an interview with Butch for the following morning, May 30.

CHAPTER 17

MAY 30, 1986

Butch later said that before leaving for the interview, his parents only told him there were "some people" he had to talk to. He presumed they were taking him to talk to a psychiatrist.

The NIS agents had rented a room at the Tapadera Motel expressly for the interview. Butch arrived accompanied by Gary Francis. Betty had to work that morning.

Freeman later described the two-hour taped interview as "low-key and non-accusatory."

During the interview, Butch was asked about the murder weapon. He said he had been told it was a filet knife with a wooden handle.

In fact, Butch had been told only that the murder weapon was "his" fishing knife. Butch concluded that the knife he usually took along on fishing trips, a knife with a wooden handle, was the knife to which the agents referred.

Butch described his knife, the one he believed to be the

murder weapon, as having a wooden handle with a thin curved blade. The knife had a broken tip and there was a chip in the wood, he said.

The knife Butch described was not the one investigators believed to be the murder weapon. But Butch's confusion was understandable. A wooden-handled fish knife had been seized from the Smith house. This was the knife Butch described. But the knife with Connie's blood on it, the alleged murder weapon, had a black plastic handle.

"Were there any other knives like that in the house?" Freeman asked, apparently prompting Butch to recall the other fish filet knife, the knife with the black plastic handle.

No, Butch replied. Not like that. But there were some steak knives in a tray on the counter next to the refrigerator.

"Were there any other kitchen knives that would cause something like this?" Freeman persisted.

"Steak knives," Butch repeated.

This response led to questions about other knives the Smiths owned, including Butch's pocket knife and a bayonet his father had brought back from Vietnam. Butch said he had not seen the bayonet in some time and believed it was locked up in an old tool box in the garage.

"Do you think whoever did this could have used that?" Freeman asked.

"I don't know. Possibility, but I wouldn't know."

Freeman later claimed that Butch was the first to mention a second murder weapon, which equated to guilty knowledge.

But according to the transcript of the May 30 interview, it was Freeman who first mentioned a second murder weapon.

"The other agents talked to you specifically about the fish knife," Freeman said. "But could there have been another knife used in all of this?"

"Yes, I suppose so," Butch replied. "Any number of those knives could have been used."

Freeman then asked Butch if he'd heard any unusual noises the night of the killings.

"Just your regular military base sounds. Dogs barking. Cars driving. People screaming."

During this same interview with Freeman, Butch was asked to "visualize" his experience of seeing Connie's body. Butch had told the agents he saw Connie's body when he veered through the living room on his way out of the house after seeing Sharon's body.

"I know it's something you don't want to think about, and you said earlier you want to put it out of your mind," Rodgers told Butch. But it was important, the agent said, that Butch recall what he had seen.

"Maybe you might help us explain how something got moved from the way you remember it," Rodgers said.

But Butch seemed confused about what he had seen, or imagined he had seen, five years earlier.

"I saw a slice across her neck," Butch said of Connie. I thought – I'm not sure but I thought – I saw one going straight down."

Rodgers repeated, "Straight down? From the neck straight down?"

Butch nodded yes.

He described Connie as wearing a purple nightgown pulled down to her ankles.

The agent asked if Connie were wearing shoes or socks and Butch answered no.

But it was Sharon, not Connie, who was wearing a nightgown, a blue one that appeared purple where it was stained with blood. Connie's wound did not go "from the neck down" but from the genitals up to the neck. And the girl had been wearing both shoes and socks.

Rodgers brought up the scratches Butch had the morning of the killings.

"You had cut yourself somehow," Rodgers said. "You want to tell us about that?"

Butch then reiterated his explanation for the cut he had on his wrist in 1981, saying it resulted from his pressing a jelly jar into the trash can.

Rodgers asked if he'd also had a cut on his face. Butch's cousin Tommy had told agents in 1981 that Butch cut his face while putting together a kit model. But by 1986, Butch had forgotten the cut and how he got it.

At one point, Rodgers suddenly asked Butch if he had any idea why the murders had been committed.

"No," Butch responded.

"No idea at all?" Rodgers persisted.

"You have something somebody isn't telling me?" Butch said.

"Do you have any idea who did it?"

"I know for sure it wasn't me. No," Butch replied.

The agents then coaxed Butch to hypothesize about details of the killings.

After asking if Tyler was a heavy or light sleeper – to which Butch responded "light" – Freeman asked Butch if Tyler might have awakened during the murders.

"Could have," Butch replied.

The agents then asked about Tyler's size and whether he could have been forcibly taken into Lorrie's room.

Butch said he and Tyler were about the same size. He agreed that Tyler might have been carried into Lorrie's room, adding that he didn't remember seeing Tyler go there to sleep. When he last saw Tyler alive, Butch said, he was stretched out on the couch in the living room.

Freeman asked Butch to picture in his mind a "for instance" of how the killings happened.

Butch responded: "The assailant came in and after he killed my Aunt Sharon and Tyler woke and saw it – the dude figured he had a witness and had to get rid of him – killed Tyler downstairs, Connie walked in and then he took care of her and took Tyler upstairs and put Connie on the couch."

It is unclear why the agents introduced the scenario of Tyler being "forcibly taken to Lorrie's room." But, as was typical of Butch, he immediately picked up on the suggestion.

It was not, however, a scenario that suited the crime scene. In light of the physical evidence, investigators concluded that all three victims were killed where they lay.

At one point early in the investigation, agents suspected Tyler had been murdered because he came downstairs and saw the killer. The killer, agents speculated, was someone Tyler knew, someone who was able to accompany the boy back upstairs and convince him nothing was amiss.

However, the killer would have been well-spattered with blood after killing Sharon Sager and it seemed unlikely that Tyler would have gone back to sleep after such an alarming sight.

Freeman asked Butch how the killer might have cleaned up.

Butch suggested there was an abundance of rags in the garage. There was no evidence, however, that the killer entered the garage, much less removed anything.

In the interview, Butch was asked how the killer could have disposed of the knife.

"If he was smart, he would walk out of the house with it and get rid of it," Butch replied.

When prompted for details, Butch said the best place would be a swampy area about a mile away.

Knowing it would have been difficult for Butch to reach the area and return in the time frame suggested by the crime scene, the agents asked Butch if the killer might have driven or ridden a bike.

Butch did not pick up on that line of thought.

The agents then turned to what they suspected to be the motive: Butch's relationship with Connie.

"Do you think she knew some secrets?" Freeman asked. "Or was about to tell some secret?"

"I wouldn't know," Butch replied.

"What kind of information would be that important that someone would want her dead?" Freeman asked.

After a bit more prodding, Butch said, "Blackmail, fraud, I don't know."

Freeman then asked Butch if the murders might have been sexually motivated. Butch said they could have been, but when asked for an example, said he couldn't give one.

Freeman next broached the subject of Tyler's phone call to his father, Dennis Dash, made the day before the murders, in which Dash said Tyler had told him that he caught Butch "in bed" with Connie.

Butch told Freeman and Rodgers he didn't know about any phone call, either between Tyler and his father or Sharon and Tyler's father.

"Did Tyler know anything about Connie maybe he could have told his father?" Freeman asked.

"I don't know," Butch replied.

"Had Connie been doing anything wrong in the neighborhood?"

"No."

"Is it possible Connie may have been experimenting at all with boyfriends and sexual matters?" Freeman asked.

"I doubt it."

"Why?"

"Connie was a pretty strait-laced girl," Butch said. "She didn't worry about boyfriends or that stuff. She was more worried about her Barbie dolls and me stepping on ants."

Butch explained that Connie didn't like to see him step on ants and would demand of her brother, "What did that ant do to you?"

He denied that Connie had ever discussed sexual matters with him, saying she probably would talk about that with Lorrie or her mother.

When pressed for examples of dissension in the family, Butch said Lorrie and Connie had had a fight the day before the murders about who was to load the dishwasher.

The sisters had argued again later and Connie had stormed off down the street, he said. She was lured back by Tyler and Butch with the promise of a bowl of ice cream.

After a few more questions, Rodgers told Butch that the reason for the interview was to find out if he was involved in the crimes.

"Let me ask you, right to the point," Rodgers said. "Were you involved in these deaths?"

"No, I was not," Butch replied.

"OK. Why could you have not been involved?"

"Why?"

"Yes."

"Because I don't have the guts or the balls to do something

like that," Butch said. "My subconscious would drive me bananas. I can't do nothing wrong without admitting to it."

Butch waffled a bit when Rodgers followed with questions about whether he ever told lies.

Rodgers then returned to the subject of the knife.

"Do you think that your filet knife, that was believed to have been used, was the only knife used?"

"From what I have heard, I doubt it."

"Why do you say that?"

"I don't know if you told me, but somebody told me that Connie's ribs were cut in two and there's no way that knife did that," Butch said.

Connie's ribs had not actually been cut. It was the cartilage connecting her ribs that had been penetrated by her chest wound.

Rodgers then asked Butch to describe various weapons, such as bayonets and hunting knives, that might have been used in addition to the filet knife.

"You think your filet knife was not used at all?" Rodgers asked.

"It was missing. I don't know."

Asked if anyone else had discussed the knife with him, Butch said, "Jones did. He tried to get me to admit I used that knife. He was kind of trying to put words into my mouth."

Butch said he had lied repeatedly to Jones, often "just to aggravate him and watch him bounce himself off the wall."

He gave Jones wrong information, Butch said, "because he kept screaming at me and I just got so pissed off that I'd tell him anything that came into my head."

Butch admitted to lying about having the shotgun the night of the killings. He also admitted to Rodgers that he had, indeed, nearly confessed to the killings several months after they happened.

"I got so sick and tired of everybody picking on me I figured if I admitted it, they would leave me alone," Butch said.

He explained that he decided not to confess because "I thought about it. Thought about living the rest of your life behind bars for something you didn't do."

Then the agents asked Butch if he could have committed the crimes and not remembered it. He said he doubted it.

The interview returned to more general questions about events the evening before the murders.

During a break, when Butch stepped out of the room to get a soda, the agents discussed with Francis the possibility of Butch taking a polygraph test. Francis was amenable to what he later said he thought would be a decisive proceeding.

An agent later told another agent: "The only reason we got the man (Butch) to take the polygraph was we told the mother's husband, this kid is a serial (killer) profile. He'll kill again. We don't know what made him snap but he's going to snap again."

But Francis didn't need to pressure Butch into taking the polygraph. He readily agreed.

Getting Butch to take a polygraph had been the agents' intent all along. Arrangements for the test had been made several days before. An NIS polygraph specialist, Robert Dortsch, had been flown in from Bremerton, Wash. This agent had been at the restaurant during the previous night's dinner but had not been introduced to the Francises.

Betty later said she and Francis had been assured the polygraph examiner would be "neutral," not an NIS agent.

The Ontario Police Department had agreed to allow agents use of their soundproof polygraph room.

CHAPTER 18

POLYGRAPH

After the motel interview, Francis and Butch had lunch and then drove to the police station. They were met by Betty, who was off work by then.

Butch and Francis were escorted to the back of the police station, where they were frisked. Butch then returned to the lobby, where he waited while Francis and Betty were taken to the examination room. The couple were advised how the polygraph worked and what questions Butch would be asked.

Satisfied with the proceedings, the Francises withdrew and Butch was hooked up to the polygraph machine.

Dortsch did several preliminary examinations of Butch, using the same questions he would ask during the actual test.

If Butch and his parents hoped the test would prove his innocence once and for all, they were gravely disappointed. According to Dortsch, Butch's responses to the incriminating questions indicated he was lying.

There is no universal response to a polygraph question that indicates a person is lying. Polygraph examiners simply measure the difference between the way the subject reacts to questions about the crime and the way he reacts to questions that are not about the crime.

When an examiner says a subject's response to a question indicates deception, the examiner really is saying the subject has responded much more strongly to that particular question than to others.

As a kind of measuring stick, the examiner asks three kinds of questions: questions concerning the crime; unrelated but provocative questions that may tempt the subject to lie; and irrelevant questions.

An example of a provocative question is: Did you ever steal anything? If the subject answers no, the examiner may decide that level of response indicates deception because the examiner presumes everybody has stolen something at some time or another.

The examiner alternates relevant, provocative and irrelevant questions.

Measuring the subject's response is complicated by the fact that it is nearly impossible to tell whether a strong response is the result of deception, fear, anger or some other strong feeling. That is why examiners try to put the subject at ease by conducting several "trial runs."

That is also why the examiner always asks the subject whether he expects the examiner to ask only the questions they have already discussed. If the subject indicates he is afraid the examiner will "trick him," the examiner tries to relieve that fear because it can skew the test results.

On Butch's crucial test, the relevant questions were:

Regarding those stabbings, do you intend to answer truthfully?

Did you stab any of those people?

Did you stab any of those people at Kentucky Court?

Do you know the name of the person who stabbed those people?

The "provocative" control questions were:

131

While in Vale, did you ever think about harming someone to get even with them?

While living in Pendleton, did you ever deliberately hurt a domestic animal?

While playing baseball, did you ever deliberately injure another player?

The irrelevant questions included:

Are the doors closed?

Are the lights on?

Is today Friday?

Are you sitting down?

Is this month May?

But it must be remembered that Butch was sensitized to questions about the stabbings in a unique way. He had seen the bodies. He had seen his sister and his cousin in their coffins. And he had a psychological history of reacting intensely to stressful situations.

Even if innocent, he could not be expected to react to a polygraph in the same way as someone who had not seen the bodies.

As one investigator expressed it, "Butch would fail a polygraph if he said yes after they asked him whether the sun came up the day of the murders."

It would have been interesting to see how Butch would have responded to questions concerning the crimes that he could have answered without danger of implicating himself.

For example: Did you see Tyler's body? Was blood coming from Tyler's ear? Was there blood on Sharon Sager's nightgown?

The relevant question – did you stab Tyler or Sharon or Connie? – could then be weighed against other questions about the emotionally-charged subject.

Former Special Agent Mike Paul, himself a polygraph expert, testified in a subsequent hearing that the control questions used in Butch's test, while acceptable, were not strong enough.

A CID agent involved in the initial investigation had another interesting, and novel, explanation for why Butch might have failed the test, even if he were innocent of the killings.

"I think Butch Smith wanted to kill them. That could make a person fail a polygraph."

As illustration, the agent cited the case of a woman who was killed with a Samurai sword in the base trailer park. Suspicion fell on the woman's husband, who failed a polygraph. Additional investigation, however, exonerated the husband and revealed the real killer.

"He bombed the polygraph," the agent said of the innocent husband, "because he was tired of her running around. He wanted to kill her."

In any case, the reliability of the polygraph has been seriously questioned in recent years. Most states, including North Carolina, do not permit polygraph results to be admitted as trial evidence. Some states and federal court districts do allow admission of polygraph results but only under stipulation that both prosecution and defense agree to the admission.

And it is not only those who have reason to fear the truth who are leery of polygraphs.

"I wouldn't take one," one agent bluntly said. He explained that a fellow agent and polygraph examiner had once demonstrated to him how easily a subject's emotions can be manipulated so he appears to be lying when he is not.

Butch's test results were presented to him and his parents as definitive.

"Butch took the polygraph and failed it," according to the examiner.

When the examiner told Butch he had not answered some of the questions truthfully, Butch insisted he was innocent and told Dortsch he was leaving.

"I couldn't have done something like that," Butch exclaimed and walked to the door.

Dortsch did not physically try to stop him.

"I thought this was important to you, that you wanted to get this thing resolved," Dortsch said, coaxing Butch to stay. "We need to talk about it."

Butch returned and sat down by the polygrapher. The two

talked for several minutes more. During the conversation, the agent introduced the subject of motive, Butch's allegedly incestuous relationship with Connie.

"It was about fifteen or twenty minutes later that Butch jumped up, indicated to me in no uncertain terms that he did not do it, and ran out of the room, out of the building, onto the street," Dortsch said.

Rodgers, who was sitting outside the examination room and could hear what was going on, later testified:

"After the examination, there was a discussion between Special Agent Dortsch and Butch, during which Butch became upset. He used words to the effect 'nobody believes me' and he left the room."

Butch ran to his parents' car and got inside. According to Freeman's statement, Butch pounded on the dashboard, screaming, "He thinks I killed those people!"

Francis recalled the scene somewhat differently:

"He came running out of the police station into the lobby, crying, and out the front door. As he ran out the front door, he said, 'I believe I'm getting out of here; I'm leaving,' " Francis would later testify. "We went out to the front and I talked to him and tried to settle him down.

"I didn't know, at this point, what had happened. And he told me, 'They said I had sex with my sister. Can you believe that?' " Francis recalled.

When Francis returned to the lobby with Butch, he saw Betty standing with Dortsch. She was crying.

"I should not have let Butch do this," Betty sobbed. Francis suggested to the polygrapher that they find a more private place than the police station lobby to deal with the situation.

Betty, Francis and Dortsch went back to the examination room. The polygrapher told them Butch had failed the test and, according to Francis, they "discussed what the possibilities were."

Butch had remained in the lobby, where Freeman approached him. Freeman encouraged Butch to speak with him in private.

Freeman pressed Butch about his knowledge of Connie's

wounds, about her being disemboweled. Freeman said Butch finally admitted he had seen that Connie had been cut open.

Freeman later told a grand jury that Butch had never admitted seeing Connie's "post mortem wound" before.

Butch later would tell his lawyer that, until Lorrie explained the phrase, years after the killings, he hadn't known what "post mortem" meant.

Whether or not Butch had stumbled over semantics, the record shows that he had told several people different versions of seeing Connie's abdominal wound.

In one version, Butch told a Lejeune High School classmate that he had inadvertently sat on the cushion covering Connie's body and blood had seeped into the seat of his pants. However, no blood was found on the seat or any other part of Butch's pants and there was a footprint, not blood, on the upper side of the vinyl cushion covering Connie's body.

To others, Butch denied ever seeing his sister's body until the funeral.

At that point during the May 30 interview, Butch became very agitated, according to Freeman, and requested counsel. Freeman ended the interview.

Francis' first reaction to the test results was anger at the polygrapher. He questioned whether the test had been objectively administered. He and Dortsch had a somewhat heated argument until they agreed, according to Dortsch, that any further discussion would be "beating a dead horse."

Betty too was upset that, once again, her son was being accused of the murders. She told the agents they could never interview Butch or his family again.

But Freeman considered whether he needed Betty's cooperation at all. He had spotted another way to get to Butch. Gary Francis. Despite Francis' anger at the polygraph examiner, Freeman sensed that Francis could be persuaded to cooperate.

Freeman called Francis at work from Camp Lejeune 10 days after the disastrous polygraph. Francis called Freeman back the next day,

Francis may have had shattering rows with his stepson, but he had consistently supported Butch's innocence for years. The polygraph results irreparably damaged that support.

The polygraph also served to test the durability of the Francises' already fragile marriage. In that respect, too, the test result would be failure.

Betty later said Francis did not confide in her the details of his conversations with Freeman. But he seemed unusually concerned about Butch's presence in the house.

"He was going to truck school and he took Butch with him so Butch would not be home while he was gone," Betty later testified.

"And why did he do that?" she was asked.

"Because he didn't want him in the house with the kids or me."

"Now, at that point did you have any apprehension or fear of Butch?"

"No, I thought it was absolutely ridiculous," Betty replied. After the polygraph exam, Butch asked his mother if he should see a lawyer. The Francises decided they could not afford one. But Francis assured Butch that, "if it came to a point where he needed a lawyer, then we would get one."

Freeman got Francis to agree to persuade Betty to meet with NIS agents again. The meeting took place June 29, 1986, one month after the polygraph.

Freeman and Special Agent John Dill met with Betty and Gary for dinner. This time, Butch was not included.

Hoping to win Betty's cooperation, the agents told her what she later described as the "gory details," the same details Freeman already had told Francis that supposedly pointed to Butch as the killer.

Francis claimed he had been told that a fingerprint found on the murder weapon was Butch's, that FBI profiles and psychiatric tests not only identified Butch as the killer, but indicated he would kill again.

To get Betty to allow agents to interview Butch again, Francis later said, he told her that "in light of the information that was passed to me, I could not afford, with three of my own children and one other child of hers in our household, to take a chance, to just blow it off and stick my head in the sand.

I convinced her to cooperate, to whatever extent she felt she could," Francis said.

Betty later insisted Francis had told her to cooperate or the marriage was over.

Francis said he had promised Betty that "if she didn't pull her head out of the sand and cooperate to an extent that would help get to the bottom of this, that I was going to remove my children from our household."

Betty's years of faith in her son's innocence began to give way to doubts. She was alarmed by Francis' conviction that Butch posed a threat to his step-siblings. Although Butch had lived with his stepbrothers and stepsister for years, Betty absorbed her husband's uneasiness. She was fond of her stepchildren, particularly the youngest, and never would have wished them any harm.

And Betty knew her third marriage was at the breaking point. She agreed to bring Butch to an interview with NIS agents the following day, June 30.

CHAPTER 19

RENEWED INTERROGATION

Francis had decided not to tell Butch he would be taking him to another interview with NIS agents. Instead, he said they would be going into town the next morning in hope of finding Butch a job.

Butch got up early and dressed for a job interview. But he sensed something was amiss, his stepfather knew.

"We were several blocks away from the motel when he said, 'We're not going to look for a job, are we?' I said no. I said the NIS was there and that they wanted to talk to him. And he said, 'I knew that.' "

"Well, then, you shouldn't be surprised," Francis told him. Francis later recalled Butch asking him, "Do you got my lawyer?"

"No. We don't know yet if you need one."

If he wanted a lawyer, Francis was sure the agents would arrange for him to have one.

Then Francis took on a stern attitude. He, Betty and the agents did not feel Butch had been completely truthful during previous interviews, he said, and they wanted the truth.

"We're going to get to the bottom of this today," Butch later recalled Francis telling him.

The agents had arranged that this interview, like the previous one, would be held at the Tapadera Motel. Before Butch went into the room to be interrogated, Francis told his stepson he loved him and that he would support him, no matter what. Francis waited across the hall.

Betty, the two agents and Butch participated in the interrogation. Betty sat at a small table across from her son.

The agents' goal was to extract a confession. The Francises' goal was to end an intolerably unsettling part of their lives. In the end, the Francises would fall painfully short of their goal. The agents would succeed in theirs.

Before the afternoon of June 30 was over, Butch would indeed confess. But to judge the credibility of that confession, one must consider the interrogation that preceded it.

Although Butch had never objected to an interview being taped, and the May 30 interview had been taped, this one was not. Both agents took notes.

The agents began by quizzing Butch about inconsistencies in previous statements, some of them made five years earlier.

"Of particular interest," Freeman would later tell a grand jury, "we had witnesses who put Butch in the window of the second story bedroom at around midnight or one o'clock in the morning the night of the murders. He was observed in the window with binoculars peering down at his sisters in the car. He denied that. He denied he'd been in the window. He denied that he'd had binoculars."

But Freeman's grand jury testimony concerning the time of the binoculars episode would differ from his testimony at another court hearing. At an earlier hearing, Freeman had been asked if statements Butch made during the June 30 interrogation were inconsistent. Freeman had replied:

"Inconsistent with his earlier statements, inconsistent with witness' statements who had described seeing him around 2:00

a.m. Butch denied that he had been up at 2:00 a.m., stating the witnesses must be mistaken."

He also would testify at another hearing that Butch had been looking through the binoculars at 2:00 or 3:00 a.m.

But Freeman's testimony about the time of the binoculars incident was mistaken. No witnesses put Butch in the window, with or without binoculars, at 2:00 a.m.

Lorrie did say Butch was looking at the car through the binoculars at 11:45 p.m.

By the June 30, 1986 interview, Butch may have forgotten the 1981 binoculars incident. There was little reason for him to deny it. Chris Sager told investigators the day after the murders that both he and Butch had been looking through the binoculars at the girls playing cards in the car – before midnight.

During the June 30 interview, Freeman pressed Butch about the binoculars. The agent produced a crime scene photograph showing binoculars on the bedroom dresser in Connie's room. Betty Francis immediately identified them as Butch's.

"So, she cornered him," Freeman later testified. "She accused him at that time of lying. 'Why would you lie about the binoculars, Butch? What are you saying? You know you have binoculars.' He denied that. He said, 'Well, my binoculars, they don't even work.'

"She confronted him again. 'Of course they work. I still have them. They still work.' He never acknowledged that he'd been in the window, but he just quit denying that he'd been in the window," Freeman said.

More damning, according to Freeman's subsequent grand jury testimony about the June 30 interrogation, was Butch's being the first to mention the possibility of a second knife as a murder weapon.

But on the subject of second knives, Agent Freeman seemed to contradict himself before the grand jury. He testified both that the filet knife found next to Tyler's body was the murder weapon – and that it could not have inflicted the horrendous wound Connie suffered.

During the grand jury, Freeman would tell the court the

murder weapon had been found. He would describe it as a "thin-bladed fish filet knife with a broken tip."

The judge would ask if experts had determined whether such a knife could have made the fatal wounds.

"Yes," Freeman would reply. "Experts have looked at it and feel that that very well could be the weapon used. Additionally, her (Connie's) blood was found on the knife."

But it was Butch's alleged guilty knowledge of another murder weapon that served as the lever to elicit a confession during the June 30 interview.

Freeman would testify to the grand jury that Butch had brought up something at this interview that had never been mentioned elsewhere, another knife. He would testify:

"We were particularly interested because of the filet knife being a fragile, somewhat, you know, thin-bladed knife (that) could not have cut through the ribs of Connie Smith. Butch brought that up during this interrogation. He's the one who brought up, 'It couldn't have been – that knife couldn't have been used to kill those people.'

"So, his mother confronted him with that: 'You know, Butch. You're the first person who's said that. You're the first person who's said there's been a second knife at any time.' So, again, he was on the spot for it."

But it was not the first time a second knife had been mentioned. By a long shot. During an interview in September 1981, Butch described disturbing dreams about the slayings. In his dreams, he said, a mustached killer used a military bayonet.

Butch's conclusion in 1981 that the killer had used a bayonet was logical. He knew from newspaper stories that the victims' throats had been cut and that one of them had been "disemboweled."

Betty and Butch were questioned about a variety of knives in 1981. Several knifes of various sorts were seized from the Smith residence. It was natural that Butch and others who were unfamiliar with details of the investigation speculated about what kind and how many knives had been used in the crimes.

Within the Camp Lejeune community, knives were commonplace, used both in military field exercises and in recreational activities. It would have been reasonable for anyone to conclude that a bayonet was a more likely murder weapon than a fish filet knife.

Freeman himself had raised the possibility of a second weapon twice during the May 30 interrogation.

And National Guard recruiter McMorris later would say that he remembered telling Butch a filet knife couldn't have produced such wounds as Butch described. That discussion took place in McMorris' office, weeks before Butch was interrogated by Freeman and Rodgers.

But the issue of the second knife was treated as guilty knowledge on Butch's part during the June 30 investigation.

Betty urged Butch to be truthful. "You've got to take responsibility for your actions if this family is going to continue as a family," she insisted.

The agents then began a curious phase of questioning intended to connect Butch to a nylon fiber that had been found embedded in Connie's blood on the murder weapon.

According to Agent Dill's notes, he asked Butch if he had a pair of nylon gloves of any kind.

Butch said he did not.

Betty contradicted him, saying there had been, indeed, nylon batting gloves at the house.

After insisting that he played soccer and not baseball, Butch finally admitted he knew there were batting gloves in the house.

The entire line of questioning was conjectural, however. No fabric gloves were taken as evidence after the murders, nor were any found in subsequent searches of the area.

Butch later told his attorney that he and Lorrie both had owned batting gloves. But his were leather with the fingers cut off. Lorrie's softball gloves may or may not have been nylon. But they would have been much too small for Butch's hands.

The question of the gloves later would become crucial.

Prosecutors would use the nylon fiber and its purported origin in a batting glove to corroborate Butch's alleged confession.

Freeman later would testify that an unidentified bloody fingerprint, covered by some sort of nylon fabric was found on the doorknob to Butch's room the day of the murders. The implication was that the nylon fabric was a batting glove that belonged to Butch.

Had Freeman not subsequently testified about the mysterious fabric under oath, it would appear the interrogation questions were merely a ruse to elicit a confession.

At a subsequent hearing held in July of 1986, Freeman would testify:

"There was a latent print in blood on Butch's doorknob to his bedroom. That print was lifted. The entire doorknob was removed and forwarded to the lab. The lab report was returned, stating it was a fingerprint protected by a nylon-type material – no ridges. No identifiable print could be raised from that."

At this stage, the fabric was merely a "nylon-type" material. But this testimony raises questions about more than fiber content.

A latent impression, by definition, includes some evidence of the ridges that distinguish a print from, say, the end of a stick. If a latent print in blood was on that doorknob, there were ridges. No ridges, no print.

By the time Freeman would testify before a grand jury in 1987, the story would have changed a bit.

"Yes, there was a bloody print found on the doorknob to the room Butch was sleeping in. When examined by the lab, there was no detail to identify it as a fingerprint but rather a print covered by nylon," Freeman said.

Freeman would reiterate this information at a 1987 detention hearing: "The bloody fingerprint, lacking sufficient detail to be identified as the fingerprint found at the scene, was described by the lab as having been covered by nylon."

Freeman was mistaken. The alleged fabric and fingerprint were never documented or suggested by any lab report. The SBI laboratory report concerning the door knob on Butch's bedroom door does not mention a fingerprint or fabric. It merely says blood found on the doorknob was Tyler's.

There was a nylon fiber on the filet knife found with Tyler's body. But Freeman was mistaken about its location.

"The knife recovered in the bedding with Tyler Dash had a nylon fiber, a single fiber, on the handle," Freeman would testify at a hearing.

According to the NIS evidence custody document, the fiber was on the knife blade – not the handle.

Tying conjectured fabric and fingerprint and genuine nylon fiber to each other and to Butch would be difficult if not impossible.

But it would be essential that Butch's confession be corroborated if it were to be ruled admissible in court.

The nylon fiber found on the knife could have been from an unlimited number of sources. The fiber was never compared to any gloves from the Smith residence because the only gloves seized were a pair of leather military gloves.

What agents appeared to have done was to take a fiber from an unidentified source and conjecture how it might be tied to Butch. The only three fabric samples sent to the FBI laboratory for comparison with the nylon fiber found on the knife blade were from the T-shirt Connie was wearing, the nightgown Sharon Sager was wearing and a bit of upholstery fabric from the couch where Connie died. The fiber on the knife matched none of them.

But during the June 30, 1986 interview, Butch's inability to answer his interrogators' questions, including his mother's, about the batting gloves unnerved him.

For the first time, his mother was siding with those who believed he was guilty. Butch did not have the emotional resources to contend with the situation and began to withdraw into more frequent silences.

It was at this stage of the interview, after Butch ostensibly lied about the "nylon" batting glove, that the NIS agents broached the topic they believed to have been Butch's motive, incest.

During subsequent grand jury testimony, Freeman would say agents had suspected an incestuous relationship existed, not only between Butch and Connie, but between Butch and his mother.

"It was something that we had maybe suspected or felt

strongly about all during the investigation because of her actions, her support of her son when, you know, he was obviously a prime suspect."

In other words, investigators felt Betty's refusal to believe her son was guilty might indicate an unnatural sexual relationship.

To further explain this suspicion, Freeman paraphrased some of Betty's remarks made to her son during the June 30 interrogation, remarks that to most observers would hardly point to incest, but would explain why Butch must have felt bitterly rejected.

"At this point," Freeman recalled of the interview, "she confronted him with statements to the effect, 'Butch, I'm your mother. I've taken care of you all your life. You're 20 years old, you haven't got a job, you don't have a driver's license, you don't have any money. I take care of you. You know, how long are we going to do this? How long are you going to be my son? You know, you have to have your own life. I have to have my own life.'

"You know," Freeman continued, "Even though the actual act of an incestuous relationship was never brought up, it was – certainly appeared that way as a result of the conversations."

But it was not an allegedly incestuous relationship between Butch and his mother that prosecutors would contend provided a motive for the murders. The prosecution would allege that Sharon Sager, Tyler and Connie died because of a peculiar lover's triangle centering on Butch's incestuous relationship with Connie.

So convinced were the agents that such a relationship existed, they tried to goad Butch at one point by telling him Connie's underpants were found in Tyler's hand.

Agent Dortsch had broached the subject of incest during the May 30 polygraph examination a month earlier and Butch had had one month in which to try and reconcile Tyler's accusation with events he remembered.

According to Agent Dill's statement, Butch was asked during the June 30 interview if he remembered Tyler calling his father the day of the murders. Dill later testified:

"Butch immediately and positively responded 'yes', and – without further question – stated he (Tyler) called his father and told him 'he had caught me in bed twice with Connie.'

"When asked to explain, Butch said his Aunt Sharon had caught Tyler and Connie in the upstairs bathroom (the connotation being they were sexually involved) and that Sharon was dragging Tyler downstairs and 'screaming at him.'

"Butch said Tyler asked if he could call his father and when Sharon agreed, she said (according to Butch) that he (Tyler) had caught Butch in bed with his own sister.

"When Butch was asked why Tyler would say this in the face of apparently just being caught in a sexual situation by the person (Sharon) placing the call and apparently standing right there, Butch replied he did not know.

"He said Sharon was shouting at him (Tyler) because he said these things.

"When asked if Sharon had caught Tyler and Connie in a sexual situation or if it was something she suspected or was told, Butch said he 'guessed' she had caught them.

"He (Butch) said Sharon had talked about the situation with Connie, the conversation having taken place in the laundry room of the home during the above-described time frame."

But Freeman's version of this phase of the June 30 interview differs from Dill's. According to Freeman, it was the agents who told Butch about Tyler calling his father:

"We brought it to his attention that the victim, Tyler Dash, had called his father – Tyler's father – the night of the murders and told his father that he, Tyler, had observed Carlton in bed with his sister," Freeman said.

Freeman said Butch responded that Tyler had lied to try and get him in trouble.

Again, Betty entered into the interrogation of her son. According to Freeman, Betty asked "other questions about that situation." He did not record what these questions were or Butch's responses.

"Is that what this is all about?" Betty finally demanded of Butch. "The murders – was it about keeping me from finding out?"

146

According to Dill's statement, Butch denied that.

But in Freeman's subsequent testimony to a grand jury, he would neglect to mention Butch's denial.

Lawyer Bogdanos would ask Freeman what happened after Butch's mother "confronted" him and Freeman would reply:

"The room became silent. Butch hung his head. No words were spoken. Everybody remained silent for what seemed an eternity. It was probably 45 seconds."

Then, according to Freeman, Butch let out a long sigh. "Butch's mother then asked him, 'Do you want me to leave the room?' He said yes. Betty Francis left the room.

The agents interpreted his desire for his mother to leave as an indication he was ready to confess.

But there was another explanation.

During a later hearing, defense attorney Richard Cannon would ask Agent Dill:

"But you were assuming at that point that he was asking her to leave so he could get it off his chest. Is that correct?"

"Yes," Dill replied.

"Isn't it also equally likely that he could have been wanting to get her off his back?" Cannon snapped.

CHAPTER 20

CONFESSION

Agents began questioning Butch after Betty left the motel room on the afternoon of June 30.

It is not clear why, if they believed Butch wanted Betty to leave because he was ashamed to talk about his relationship with Connie, that the agents did not follow up with questions about this after Betty left.

The two agents' accounts of Butch's next remarks differ significantly. Freeman later would tell a grand jury:

"I continued asking Butch, without breaking the mood because of the silence, what happened. He said he remembered now that he must have done it."

Freeman said Butch was then asked to describe what happened.

Dill's notes, however, record a different version:

"Mrs. Francis departed. At this point Butch had agreed he 'could have' committed the crime, but stated he could not remember having done so. Butch was then asked how he thought the crime would have been committed."

Both agents agreed that Butch's responses were in the third person.

"Butch said the killer would have gotten the knife from the kitchen, killed Sharon Sager and then gone upstairs and killed Tyler Dash," Dill said in his statement.

"When asked about Connie Smith, he replied to the effect that she must have walked into the house and found the killer and 'he naturally had to kill her to keep her quiet' or words to that effect."

Butch was not asked to explain why Connie, seeing a blood-drenched killer, did not scream, but instead proceeded to the couch where she lay down and went to sleep. Because of the layout of the house, it would be impossible for someone to come in the front door and not see a person standing on the stairs.

Investigators agreed that Connie Smith was killed while sleeping. She died not because she had witnessed anything but simply because she was the victim of a maniacal fury.

At that point in the interview, Freeman asked Butch if he now remembered committing the crime.

According to Agent Dill's statement, Butch then said, "I guess I did it."

Freeman would testify later that Butch said something much more positive: "I remember now. I did it."

Butch was then asked how he had done it.

"I just went off and started slicing up people," he said.

Freeman asked him to explain.

Butch said he got a knife from the drawer in the kitchen and killed his aunt first, making a "figure four" shaped wound in her throat. He then went upstairs and killed Tyler. He was walking down the stairs to get rid of the evidence when Connie came in the front door.

According to Dill's statement, Butch said he waited until she lay down on the couch and went to sleep and then he killed her.

Because the interrogation was not taped, it is impossible to reconstruct it precisely. According to Freeman's later testimony at a grand jury hearing, Butch – even after saying "I remember now. I did it" – still refused to answer in the first person.

"He agreed to answer the questions in the third person. We could ask questions, 'Butch, what would the killer have done next?' He would tell us. So, we went through the entire crime scene in the third person," Freeman said.

But when Freeman asked what had happened after the killings, Butch replied, "I got rid of the evidence."

When asked where, Butch said he walked to a bridle path with a bridge behind the stables at Camp Lejeune. There, he said, he wrapped the knife and the nylon batting glove he had worn in his bloody T-shirt, put a large rock on the bundle, tied it securely and threw the bundle into the swamp to the right of the bridge.

Butch's explanation of how he got rid of the evidence presented a host of problems. Whoever committed the three murders likely was liberally covered with blood. Lightly-stained towels left at the scene could not account for the clean-up that would have been required for the killer to move through the house without leaving a bloody trail. Other rags or towels would have been needed and none was found.

While some investigators believed that a damning indication of Butch's guilt was that no one saw anyone enter or leave the Smith apartment, neither did anyone see Butch, who, according to his confession, walked through a dense housing area, laden with bloody items, in the light of early day, at a time when many Marines were already reporting to work.

When searches after the confession turned up nothing, agents would speculate that Butch threw the bloody items in one of the neighborhood trash cans which were picked up before agents arrived on the morning of the killings.

But if that were so, why would a person who was confessing try to mislead? And why neglect to explain an important piece of evidence left at the scene, a bloody knife?

When Freeman and Dill pressed Butch about the motive for the murder and the post mortem wounds to Connie's body, he clammed up, telling them, "That's all you're going to get."

Later, Butch told his lawyer he said that because, "I couldn't give a motive and I sure-as-hell couldn't give a reason why she got all cut up."

Butch later would contend, and Freeman deny, that he was promised that if he confessed, he would be incarcerated in a mental institution instead of being sent to prison.

But in a suppression hearing held in 1987, Dill would testify: "During the conversation with Butch he was told that whoever did this needed help and I figured that he'd done it, and he was going to have to admit it before he could get on the road to get some help."

A further indication that Butch believed he would be hospitalized instead of imprisoned was his remark near the end of the June 30 interview that he hoped he would have a blond, 21-year-old female doctor.

"I'll cooperate with her," he quipped.

During that same hearing, Freeman would recall that conversation a bit differently. He said either Butch or Betty brought up an "insanity-type situation" and Butch commented, "Yeah. That would be nice. I would like to get a hospital by the sea with a blond nurse."

Butch's experience at the Duke hospital five years earlier had left a far-from-unpleasant impression of psychiatric institutions.

Dill showed Butch the waiver-of-rights form he had signed at the beginning of the interview and asked him to write a statement at the bottom of the page and sign it again. Butch wrote, "I Butch J. Francis hereby state that I now recall that I did do what I am accused of doing."

After Butch signed the statement, a triumphant Freeman left the room to set the wheels in motion for Butch's arrest. When he returned, Dill was taking down Butch's statement, this one given in the first person.

"I thought I better get it down in writing in case I change my mind," Butch told him.

The first-person version of events Butch gave the agent was as bizarre and, in many respects, as incompatible with the physical evidence as were his previous versions.

Prompted by the agents, Butch said that the afternoon before the killings, after the fracas between Sharon and Tyler, he had gone to the house of a neighborhood friend and smoked marijuana.

The agents asked if he remembered watching the movie *The Awakening* on television the night of the murders. In it, a character's throat is slashed and a mummy is cut open. Butch said he did recall the movie.

After watching it, he said, he went to bed and later got up to go to the bathroom. Butch said going to the bathroom possibly "triggered" something.

When asked if the "trigger" could have been related to the sexual situation previously mentioned, Butch said he didn't know. It's not clear from the agents' statement whether the "sexual situation" they referred to was the episode between Connie and Tyler in the bathroom, or Butch's alleged relationship with his sister.

Butch said he came downstairs, went to the kitchen drawer and retrieved a knife. He then went to Sharon's bed and cut her throat.

Asked by Dill if he remembered "the situation," Butch said, "I do recall doing it. Vaguely, but I do remember."

At the time Freeman returned to the motel room, Butch had just drawn the pattern of the cut he said he had used to kill his aunt.

On the sketch of a chin, neck and shoulders that Dill had drawn, Butch had drawn a triangular pattern, similar to a figure four. He said he revolved the knife once at the end of each point of the triangle. Such an attack was quickest and easiest, he said, because it destroys every trace of evidence "so you can't tell which knife did it."

He said he had learned how to kill in that manner from *Gung Ho* magazine.

Gung Ho, which ceased publication in the late 1980s, was a heavy-handed mercenary magazine that made *Soldier of Fortune* look effete. It is unlikely, however, that Butch had much access to it. The first issue of *Gung Ho* was published in Connecticut in March of 1981. Because it was a bi-monthly publication, only three issues had been published by August of 1981. And those first issues were sparsely distributed.

Freeman later would testify, and the prosecutor insist, that the drawings matched the victims' wounds "exactly."

However, this was not the case. The wound Butch described and drew was not the wound Sharon Sager suffered, according to the autopsy report, which itemizes several slashing cuts on her head and deep fatal slashes to her neck, each made in a left-to-right direction. It is impossible to draw a figure four or triangle with all the lines in a left-to-right configuration. And there is no indication in the autopsy report that a knife blade was "revolved" in the wound.

"I guess you want to know what I was wearing," Butch volunteered. Blue jeans, a T-shirt and a pair of soccer shoes with "turf cleats," he said.

He went on to draw a slightly more accurate sketch of Tyler's wound, although he described it as "ear to ear," which it was not, having been on the left side of the victim's neck in a slightly downward direction.

Butch later told his lawyer the lines he added to Dill's sketches were sheer conjecture.

"All I saw was a big hole. I didn't know how he was cut up," Butch said.

He told the agents he put his hand over Tyler's mouth to prevent him from screaming.

He came downstairs as Connie was coming in the front door, he said, and he was thinking, "it's like a dream that's finally fitting together. I hope I was not laughing because that would make it harder to deal with."

Butch later told his lawyer he spoke of laughing because "I envisioned myself being a very sick individual at that time."

Butch said he stood on the stairs, watched Connie lie down on the couch and, 10 minutes later, went over and did the same to her that he had done to Tyler.

He then "went for a walk," he said. Asked where, he said he walked down the court, down the street to the right and about 500 yards into the woods. He said he wrapped "my knife with my T-shirt, put a big rock in it, tied it up nicely, threw it to my right into the swamp and watched it sink. Then I ran home and cleaned up my mess."

How had he cleaned up?

He used a wash rag out of the bathroom, he said, a red wash rag.

Asked what exactly he had cleaned, Butch blurted out, "My big mess – How am I supposed to know? All I know, it was big."

And what had he done with the wash rag?

"I put it in the laundry. Who would check a red washcloth?" He told the agents he then went to bed.

Butch's attorney later would say it was significant that Butch did not mention taking a shower. No blood was found in the shower and only minute traces in the apartment's sinks. And even a vigorously flushed drain usually will show evidence of blood, according to the SBI. Could the killer have appeared clean less than two hours after the murders without having taken a shower?

The agents then asked Butch about his feelings when he awoke the morning after the murders.

"I didn't know I did it," he said. "I had calmed down." Butch asked the agents if he would be sent to a mental institution for treatment. The agents' notes do not include their response.

Once again, the agents asked Butch if he remembered Connie's post mortem wound. "No. I must have really been out of it."

Asked again where he learned how to use the knife, Butch repeated that it was from *Gung Ho*. At this point, according to the agent's statement, Butch reached into the air, simulating putting a hand over a person's mouth from the rear and then stabbing down into the throat of an imaginary victim.

However, the victims had been killed from the front, as evidenced by Tyler's and Sharon's defense wounds.

Prodded by the agents, Butch then described in greater detail the route he allegedly took into the woods to dispose of the murder weapon:

"Go to the main entrance to Watkins Village. There's an

electric generator or small power plant. There is a road that splits the woods that is a maintenance road to the power lines. Follow that road behind the horse stables. As you approach the horse stables, by the manure pile, there is a riding trail. Follow that trail all the way down to a small man-made bridge. Stop in the middle of the bridge, turn to the right, look straight ahead and good luck."

After this extraordinarily detailed recollection of a heavily-traveled area he had not visited in five years, Butch said:

"I would go find it for you, but that would be too much on my head."

He then remarked, "I must be a good kid because I had all kinds of people convinced I didn't do it."

The agents asked Butch to describe the knife used in the attacks. He described a foot-long knife with a triangular blade. He drew a picture of a saw-like weapon on Dill's notes.

After that he said he wanted to change the topic to his life in Oregon, his friends and his leisure activities.

If Butch were innocent, how did he ad lib a detailed, if illogical, account of the killings so spontaneously? Had he imagined the events so repeatedly that he could replay them on cue? There may be another explanation.

Former NIS agent Michael Paul testified at a hearing in 1988 that Butch's confession was little more than a recitation of what he had been told in 1981.

"That was the hypothesis that was presented during the interrogation (in 1981). You did this because of this. This is what happened and that's why you did it."

Years later, Butch would say of his confession: "It was just like you're up in an airplane in a bad storm. And you're the solo pilot and they talk you through it."

Later that afternoon, Butch was arrested by the Malheur County Sheriff's Department in Ontario. He was probably unaware that Malheur is French for misfortune. The next day he was transported to Portland for an initial hearing. Afterward, accompanied by federal marshals, he was flown to North Carolina and taken to the Cumberland County Jail in Fayetteville.

He had no idea that he had stepped into a legal nightmare that would consume the next five years of his life.

CHAPTER 21

LEGAL BATTLE BEGINS

Prosecutor Matthew Bogdanos anticipated the trial of Butch Smith with a crusader's fervor.

The lawyer appointed to represent Butch shared Bogdanos' devotion to the law but not his eagerness for a trial. Richard Cannon, just three years out of law school at Campbell University in Buies Creek, N.C., resembled a young Jimmy Carter and had a similar soft-spoken diffidence.

He had signed up for the federal list of attorneys willing to represent indigent clients for the same reason many novice lawyers do. He needed the business. He just squeaked onto the list before the law was changed to require an apprenticeship of those appointed to federal cases.

Most federal indigent cases involve drugs and firearms, although they may include racketeering, bank fraud, environmental violations and maritime law.

When the federal public defender's office in Raleigh

assigned Cannon to the Butch Smith case, his experience at that level was relatively scant.

The sandy-haired young lawyer's federal cases had been limited to simple pleas. These involved such matters as contested wills, and one case in which Cannon represented the "wheel man" in an armed robbery. He'd had no superior court trial experience.

So surprised was Cannon at being appointed to the Smith case that he immediately called North Carolina Federal Public Defender John Howard, Oregon Federal Public Defender Paul Petterson and U.S. Magistrate Wallace Dixon. He wanted to confirm that the appointment wasn't some kind of bureaucratic bungle.

He was told not to worry, that it was only a juvenile case, one that did not include the death penalty.

Coincidentally, Dixon had been an assistant U.S. attorney who had participated in the decision not to prosecute Butch in 1981 because of insufficient evidence.

Cannon was advised to call Stephen Sady, who worked for Petterson in Oregon.

Sady agreed that Butch must be prosecuted as a juvenile. Sady spoke from experience. He had just finished a case involving a youth accused of committing a crime on federal land – an Indian reservation.

Sady advised Cannon to do nothing. A juvenile case must be heard within 30 days. If Cannon filed even a single motion, the 30-day period could be extended. If the clock ran out, Butch must be released.

"It was Steve's – and my – position that the only difference between 1981 and then was the confession, if you can call it that," Cannon said later. "I'm not sure it rises to that level."

Sady warned Cannon that the government might try to have Butch tried as an adult.

The same day, Cannon called Butch at the Cumberland County Jail and urged him to take full advantage of his right to remain silent.

The next day was Saturday, the Fourth of July. Cannon spliced another phone call to Butch between his responsibilities as a Jaycee. Greenville stages a city-wide celebration on the town commons every Independence Day. Cannon had agreed to lend a hand as hot dog hustler and bingo promoter.

Sunday, Cannon and his wife Renny drove to Fayetteville to meet Butch.

Renny, a fresh-faced brunette with the same appealing intensity as her husband, was on the faculty at East Carolina University in Greenville. She and Richard had been married less than a year.

While Renny drove, Cannon studied cases and jotted down notes. It would become something of a weekend ritual during the next two years, especially after Butch was moved to the Craven County Jail in New Bern.

"It was a choice," Cannon said. "She could go with me and we could chat, or she could just write me off for that weekend. There were so many weekends I'd be in New Bern with Butch.

"She'd give up the three hours I might talk to him so she could visit with me while we drove back and forth. Renny did an incredible amount of needlepoint during that time."

The couple took books and magazines to Butch, who was appreciative of their kindness. The following March, they would bring a cake for his 21st birthday.

Cannon and his client talked for several hours that first meeting. Instead of the bizarre individual Cannon had been led to expect, he found Butch to be boyish, pleasant and talkative. Butch seemed especially animated when talking about Carolina basketball, perhaps because he knew Cannon was a University of North Carolina graduate.

The lawyer noted that Butch was tall and slender and remarkably calm, considering his predicament.

Butch told him he had been led to believe he would be going to a halfway house or psychiatric facility – not prison.

A few days later, Cannon spoke to the Francises by phone. Gary was convinced of Butch's guilt. And Betty, too, seemed to have resigned herself to the fact that her son was a murderer.

She would later insist that Francis had manipulated her emotions until she feared Butch might harm her or Lorrie.

She told Cannon NIS agents had convinced Gary that if

Butch were tried as a juvenile or found to be mentally incompetent, he could only be held in a prison or mental institution until he was 21. And then the family would again be in danger.

Gary wanted Butch to be tried as an adult – and convicted, she said.

But Betty insisted that she still loved Butch.

To see his client tried as an adult was the last thing Cannon wanted. But already, he noted, Butch's situation was unclear. To prosecutors, his age in 1986 was more relevant than his age in 1981 when the crimes were committed.

Butch certainly was not being treated like a juvenile. His name had appeared on several documents instead of "juvenile male," as was usual in such cases. Both his picture and name had appeared in newspapers.

And the government was trying to proceed against Butch by complaint instead of a bill of information. Juvenile cases are heard by a judge in closed proceedings, based on a bill of information.

Cannon initially objected when Butch was housed in an adult cell block. But trying to accommodate Butch's juvenile status would present so many problems that Cannon was forced to relent.

Because of his age, Butch could not be housed with boys who actually were juveniles. If he were not housed with adults, the alternative would be for Butch to be in isolation, a grim situation usually reserved as punishment for jailhouse troublemakers.

And even if a suitable facility were available, it might be so far from Greenville as to make it difficult for Cannon to meet with his client.

Cannon hated to compromise on the matter because he feared it would jeopardize Butch's right to be considered a juvenile. Butch's ambiguous status already had created a curious psychological bias in those connected to the case.

He was not viewed by investigators and fellow inmates as a grown man accused of having killed three people when he was 15. He was viewed as a 20-year-old accused of killing a woman and two children.

Although the opposing lawyers had spoken several times by phone, Cannon met Bogdanos for the first time at Butch's initial appearance held July 8 in New Bern before Magistrate Charles McCotter.

Cannon succeeded in convincing McCotter to substitute a bill of information for the complaint.

Butch was ordered held in custody but Cannon arranged for him to be transferred to the brand-new Craven County jail in New Bern, nearer Greenville.

If the prosecution seemed somewhat tractable about the substitute bill of information, perhaps it was because they were planning another approach.

On July 11, 1986, the government filed a motion asking that Butch's case be transferred to adult court for trial.

Cannon filed a response saying that such a transfer violated *ex post facto* law.

A private investigator, Charles Griffin, hired to locate and interview witnesses, helped Cannon analyze the case.

Griffin, his associate, Bill Martin, and Cannon tried to measure the strength of the evidence by assuming the roles of Butch; the other suspect in the case, William Kraagman; and the mysterious "bearded man." The object was to determine which of the three made the most convincing killer.

Then the lawyer and private investigators switched roles to see if anybody could come up with a new angle.

"It seemed like there was a good case for each one having done it. And unanswered questions for each one," Griffin said later.

He reconstructed the order of the killings differently than most investigators. Connie was killed first, he speculated. The killer came in the front door, saw Connie, who in the dim light resembled her mother, and killed her. He then killed Sharon and Tyler.

In mid July, Cannon visited the crime scene and saw the evidence locker at NIS. The lawyer was impressed with the volume of evidence, which was stored in a shelf-lined vault.

Bag after bag, item after item was brought into a small room by the custodian. Cannon mulled over several still-gruesome items, including the blood-smeared cushion from the couch where Connie died. He wondered why some apparently irrelevant items, such as a stereo, had not been returned to the Smiths.

The hearing on the motion to transfer the case and a preliminary examination were held July 25, in Wilmington. To Cannon, the transfer hearing seemed to consist largely of the prosecution's demonstrating how vicious the crimes were.

"I thought it was irrelevant how bad the cuts were," Cannon recalled.

During the hearing, as in subsequent proceedings, witnesses gave an incriminating spin to physical evidence that lab reports actually had shown to be exculpatory.

In an effort to get an explanation of why, if Butch were the killer, his fingerprints were not on the bloody filet knife, Bogdanos asked NIS Special Agent Freeman, "On cross-examination you indicated that there had been no fingerprints on the filet knife. Is that correct?"

"Yes," Freeman replied.

"Did Butch give you any explanation for why you wouldn't find any fingerprints on the murder weapon?"

"He indicated he wore a baseball batting glove."

Freeman was correct in stating that Butch's prints were not on the knife. However, he neglected to add that somebody else's print was – a partial palm print on the knife handle that the FBI had been unable to identify. If the palm print had been the killer's, it indicated whoever wielded the knife had not worn a glove.

But Cannon's prime concern at this point was not to refute the prosecution's interpretations of physical evidence. His argument against the state's right to transfer was as clear and unshakable, he thought, as the *ex post facto* provision of the Constitution. That provision forbids a person from being tried under a law enacted after the crime was committed.

Two elements must be present to prove violation of *ex post facto*: the law is being applied retroactively; and the defendant is disadvantaged because of that application.

The federal Juvenile Delinquency Act that was in effect in

1981 said that a 15-year-old convicted of a crime could be imprisoned only until age 21. The 1981 law did allow juveniles age 16 or older to be tried as adults in some instances.

The prosecution was trying to transfer Butch to adult court under a 1984 amendment to that federal law. The amendment moved back the age a juvenile could be tried as an adult to 15.

Being tried under the amendment would definitely be to Butch's disadvantage. It provided for life imprisonment or the death penalty.

The government's argument was based on two cases in which individuals were tried as adults for crimes they committed as juveniles. But Cannon did not feel the cases were applicable. In both cases, the trials were delayed because the juvenile defendants jumped bail and left the court's jurisdiction for several years – until they were adults.

The prosecution also contended that juvenile laws are merely procedural, laws that tell officials how to proceed instead of dealing with the substance of a specific infraction.

Ex post facto is not violated if the law in question is merely procedural. Therefore, the prosecution argued, the change in the juvenile law which allowed a 15-year-old to be transferred to adult court could be applied to Butch's case.

Cannon argued that the kind of procedural changes that did not violate *ex post facto* were relatively insignificant things, such as the number of people comprising a grand jury. A change that would make a defendant subject to the death penalty, as opposed to imprisonment until age 21, was much more substantial than a change in procedure, Cannon argued.

The court did not agree. Judge James C. Fox granted the government's motion to transfer.

Cannon was devastated.

"Being the young, idealistic attorney I was, I felt this was wrong. The Constitution is the Constitution."

Bogdanos told Cannon an appeal was futile.

"There's no need to appeal this case," Cannon recalled Bogdanos telling him. "Whichever way the judge would have gone, the court of appeals would probably go the same way. You can't accomplish anything appealing this case."

"Well, Matt. We'll see," Cannon responded, concealing his dismay.

When he told the judge of his decision to appeal, the judge said he agreed wholeheartedly, much to Cannon's surprise.

"He was being practical," Cannon said. "To a degree, the court must answer to the local press. They are concerned about what's in the best interest of the public as well as the justice system. I remember thinking he agreed that it was an issue that needed to be taken to a higher court. That he wasn't willing to take that step."

As part of his preparation, Cannon asked Griffin, a retired Marine captain with a counterintelligence background, to interview both Betty and Butch.

"He'd talk for two hours and not say anything," Griffin recalled of his talks with Butch. "If Butch talked about Butch, it was outlandish fabrications."

Butch recounted grandiose adventures, such as the hijacking of a spy airplane he and a friend had allegedly plotted. He seemed to idolize his stepfather, Jim Smith, to a near-mythic extent, Griffin recalled.

Betty, Griffin said, was equally chatty. And equally evasive. As part of his assignment, Griffin tracked the route Butch told NIS in his confession that he had taken to dispose of the alleged murder weapon and bloodstained clothing.

Griffin thought it unlikely that a 15-year-old boy had made such a foray through dark woods along unlit, narrow paths.

"It was about seven to eight minutes each way. Why go so far?"

And the mosquitoes and snakes would deter anybody, Griffin said. "I went through there in the summer and the mosquitoes almost ate me alive."

Cannon's appeal took the case to the U.S. Fourth Circuit Court of Appeals, and he worried about how he would handle it.

"I knew even less about federal appeals than I knew about federal district court practice," he later recalled.

He learned from his adversary. As he developed his case, Bogdanos sometimes patronized him mercilessly.

"I sort of played to that," Cannon said. "I guess I tried a little of the Sam Ervin approach – the simple country lawyer technique."

But he was more than willing to make use of Bogdanos' admittedly superior experience.

"I admit I liked him," Cannon said. "You can't help but like him. And I have to say I learned a lot from him that first month. Things I hadn't thought of, his people had already researched.

"He'd call and say, 'You know, we're going to use Rule 403,' and I'd say, 'Gee. I never heard of that one.' Sometimes I was being cagey. And sometimes it was true."

By the fall, Betty and Gary Francis had separated but she continued to care for Francis' youngest child, a girl. Betty began to feel she had sacrificed her son for a marriage that had been destined to fail anyway.

"Once she got away from him and went back to New York and started piecing things together," Cannon said, "she realized there were a lot of things the government hadn't shared with her that were more favorable to Butch."

When he finally met her in person several months later, Cannon thought Betty was "chatty, likable and a little flighty."

He felt empathy for the woman who, to Cannon, seemed, typical of the military wife in many respects: "tough, a survivor who could handle herself but with no hard edges."

But that fall Cannon was not yet wholly confident of her cooperation.

"I didn't have a good feel about which way she was going to go until later in the case," he recalled.

The prosecution was equally concerned that Betty might shift back to Butch's defense.

"I was considered a hostile witness by both sides," Betty later recalled.

Cannon speculated that the prosecution wanted to keep Butch estranged from his mother in hopes that he might agree to a plea arrangement.

"Because the state knew Butch had such a strong attachment to his mother, and would pretty much do as she said, they felt as long as they could disrupt the family they could keep the pressure on Butch."

Bogdanos' view of Betty was less benign. He was annoyed by her insistence that she be shown incontrovertible evidence of Butch's guilt.

The two met at the Camp Lejeune legal office in October of 1986, four months after Butch was arrested. Their versions of the stressful meeting differ.

Betty said Bogdanos had spoken to her earlier in the week by phone and had asked to meet with her. He had agreed to show her proof of Butch's guilt, she later recalled.

"I was sitting across from him. He opened a file and said, 'Did you see what he did?' I thought he meant had I seen the house. The MPs had taken me in the house after the murders to let me get an asthma prescription one of the children needed.

"He threw these color pictures down. One was of my daughter lying on a slab at the morgue. I don't know why I thought those kinds of pictures would be in black and white. I just stared at it. I remember gagging into the trash pail.

"I must have started screaming because two MPs grabbed me. I had a few choice words for them, too. That was the cruelest thing anyone could have done."

Bogdanos said that Betty did see a crime-scene photograph but not under the circumstances she described. He said she walked into his office unannounced and demanded to see them. When he advised it was not a good idea, she insisted.

She was seated on a small red couch, he recalled. He felt pretentious and uncomfortable sitting behind his desk, officiously distant from a member of the victim's family. But his office was too small to allow him to pull up a chair.

"As I recall, she saw one picture. And it was not a bad picture. It was a faraway shot, not a shot of Connie. If she'd asked to see a picture of Connie, I would have told her to file a request through the FOI Act."

It was coincidental that the photographs were in a file on his desk, Bogdanos said.

"I remember her saying, 'Can I see my own sister?' after she saw the name on the file. After she saw, she began to cry."

By this time, Bogdanos was thoroughly exasperated by Betty's vacillation.

"One day she was convinced he was innocent. The next day she was 100 percent convinced he was guilty and she'd say, 'You've got to do something. I'm in danger and my daughter's in danger.' A week later, it would be, 'How can you persecute this innocent boy?' "

Betty was not the only family member who would claim she had been ill-used by those seeking to prosecute Butch.

Lorrie called Cannon at his office and said an NIS agent had called her the night before. During the upsetting call, Lorrie said, the agent told her she was going to jail because she refused to testify against Butch.

If Betty's statements sometimes seemed ambivalent, Butch's were even more so. And more potentially damaging.

He continued to make statements that were, at the same time, admissions of guilt and indications of innocence. He told federal marshals he didn't know whether he did it. He said there were blanks in his memory.

"From the time I went to bed until I got up is a big blank," he said.

CHAPTER 22

FEDERAL PROSECUTION

On April 11, 1987, in accordance with a court order, Butch was examined by a psychiatrist to determine if he were competent to stand trial. He was determined to be so.

The doctor, a consultant in forensic psychiatry, diagnosed mixed personality disorder. He said Butch was under considerable stress as a result of being in jail and was not likely to be dangerous to others if released on bond.

No judge was willing to take that chance.

And Cannon wasn't willing to try the case without first exhausting procedural avenues.

"My feeling," Cannon said, "was that the government's case, even with all they had, was thin. But with the photos of the crime scene, Butch wouldn't stand a chance with a jury."

Cannon would hesitate to put Butch on the stand for fear his personal appearance and unpredictable responses might prejudice a jury.

Bogdanos had a few reservations of his own. "I thought it would be a hard case. It was pretty much circumstantial. But I thought the weight of the circumstantial evidence, coupled with his numerous statements, would lead to a conviction."

The case became all-consuming for both attorneys.

"For that four- or five-year period, I lived, ate, slept and dreamed this case," Cannon said.

On May 26, 1987, the Fourth Circuit Court of Appeals agreed with Cannon and reversed the order to transfer. He was jubilant.

But it was far from over. Butch's right to be tried as a juvenile was still in jeopardy.

On July 6, the federal government dismissed the juvenile charges against Butch, and the following day a federal grand jury indicted Butch on three counts of murder.

Having failed to try Butch as an adult by shifting the case from juvenile to adult court, the prosecutor was starting anew, this time sidestepping juvenile court entirely. It was a stunning move.

Cannon was livid. "It really pissed me off. We'd finally proved our point. We'd won at the appellate level. I thought it was pure dirty tricks."

Bogdanos feigned surprise at Cannon's consternation. "You mean you'd object to a dismissal?" Cannon recalled being asked. "Why, that's tantamount to malpractice."

Only the prosecution presents its case at a grand jury. Because a grand jury hearing is closed to the public, Betty was not aware of what was said. She would have been horrified had she known Freeman's testimony implied not only an unnatural relationship between her son and dead daughter, but an unnatural relationship between her son and herself. Freeman would not repeat the allegations at subsequent hearings.

After the indictment, Cannon filed a series of motions, including one to suppress the confession as well as other statements. He contended not only that the confession had been coerced but that Butch had never been truly free to leave.

"Smith was transported to the site of the interrogation by his parents and, therefore, did not have his own transportation.

Thus, he was not 'free to leave.' His appearance at the site of the interrogation was orchestrated through the use of sub-terfuge and arranged between NIS agents and Smith's family."

Cannon also sought more discovery material.

By law, the defense is allowed access to all material the prosecution plans to present as evidence of the defendant's guilt. The prosecution also must provide the defense with material which tends to be exculpatory. The material is called "discovery."

The prosecutor is not required to relinquish his "work product" – his personal notes and trial strategies.

Bogdanos would later reassure Cannon: "Indeed, not only do you have all the material I expect to use," he wrote, "you have all the material that I might use."

By this time, Butch had made a number of undeniably incriminating remarks. The prosecution intended to make full use of them should the case come to trial.

But during the federal grand jury hearing, prosecutors also would make full use of information that, while technically cor-rect, was misleading.

When asked who found the bodies, Freeman said the defendant had. But it was Tommy who first awoke that morn-ing and told Butch that Tyler was dead. Tommy, Chris and Butch together discovered the body of Sharon Sager.

Also inaccurate was Freeman's description of Connie's post-mortem wound. Although the wound was certainly horrif-ic enough to need no embellishment, Freeman said the killer had cut through "several ribs." According to the autopsy report, the wound transected the costal cartilage of the ribs, not the ribs themselves.

Freeman also testified that Butch should not be allowed bail because a psychiatrist said in 1981 that Butch posed a threat to his family.

"His opinion at that time was that the defendant could like-ly commit further murders and that his mother could very well be the next victim."

In fact, no written profile or psychiatric evaluation of Butch identifies him as the killer, or Betty as the next victim.

FBI profiles did indicate that the perpetrator of the crimes might kill again. But, according to two agents' recollections, the profiles also indicated the crimes were committed by a person both older and stronger than Butch had been in 1981.

The grand jury indictments did include an interesting addition. It charged Butch with trying to escape from the Craven County jail in New Bern.

It was not freedom but access to a television program the inmates sought, according to Butch. Jail officials cut off the cellblock television to punish inmates for throwing food during supper. The inmates decided to crawl through an air conditioning vent into the control booth and turn the television back on themselves.

"One guy tried going through the hatch, but he was too big," Butch said. "I was the skinniest so I got the job of squeezing through and turning the television on."

He didn't get far. Butch was caught with his feet dangling out of the air conditioning vent.

Because the control booth also contained the electronic "keys" to the cellblock, a jail official initially reported the prisoners were trying to escape.

However, at a detention hearing held July 9, two days after the grand jury, Jailer John Everington corroborated Butch's version of the alleged escape and testified that Butch had created no problems while a prisoner. Everington also gave his opinion of Butch's then year-long confinement in the jail.

"There is no recreational facility. No way that they can get any fresh air. They are incarcerated without any outside activity. In my opinion, I don't think it's suitable to hold an inmate for a year or two at a time under those circumstances."

At the same hearing, Lorrie feigned a fleeting bravado.

During recesses, she and her brother made grotesque and silly faces at each other. It appeared to one observer as a defiant and inappropriate attempt to deflect rumors of estrangement.

But Lorrie had been deeply traumatized by the events of 1981.

She was extremely anxious about testifying and spoke so

softly when first on the stand that Cannon asked her to speak louder.

During direct examination, Cannon asked Lorrie if Butch had gotten into fights.

"In fights?" she responded.

"Has he ever gotten in fights before?" Bogdanos persisted.

"Of course," Lorrie said.

"You say 'of course.' What do you mean by that?"

"Doesn't everybody?" Lorrie retorted.

On cross examination, Bogdanos asked Lorrie if she remembered saying in 1981 that she was afraid of Butch because of his "strange behavior and quick temper."

Lorrie balked at replying, but, when pressed, said she had just wanted to get out of North Carolina.

Cannon later asked her to clarify her feelings on August 24, 1981.

"I was afraid of everybody," she said. "Because I didn't know who to trust and I didn't know who did it. So I didn't know if he was still out there looking for me and my mom."

During his closing remarks, the usually self-contained Cannon vented some of the outrage he felt at the grand jury allowing Butch to be indicted in the wake of the appellate decision.

"It strikes me as very odd that the government would be asking for fairness when, in actuality, it is going to do everything it can to circumvent the power of the court and the orders and decisions of this court."

He also had a few stinging remarks about the investigation. "This occurred in the middle of a Marine Corps base where you have, probably, 50,000 men who are all trained to perform the same maneuvers that the government has taken pains to show were how these murders were committed.

"There are some suspects who have been trained in those maneuvers, who had access to the duplex that night, and whose comings and goings, to this day, have never been explained."

The judge did not allow bail. But he did allow Butch to be sent to the more commodious Camp Butner near Durham for a psychological evaluation.

A few months later, in September of 1987, Butch would enjoy a wonderful respite at the psychiatric hospital at the Springfield, Mo., federal prison.

"It was like a country club with a fence," he recalled. "There was golf, racquetball and a weight room."

Interviews with prison hospital staff revealed that Butch, when confined alone, would see visions of Connie, who would sit on his bed and talk to him. He also said he conversed with a voice he called "Clyde." This voice was a great comfort to him, Butch said.

"In discussing extensively the voices and hallucinations that he had had during his incarceration, it became clear that this seemed to be more of a conscious defense mechanism to deal with the stress of prolonged solitary confinement rather than evidence of an actual psychotic disease," the psychiatrist reported.

From Springfield, Butch was sent to Nashville, N.C. It is unclear why Butch was moved there. Cannon theorized he was "set up" by investigators seeking further admission of guilt.

One of Butch's fellow inmates at the jail told authorities Butch had confessed to him. This would later be the basis of prosecutors' claims that Butch had confessed more than once.

However, felon witnesses are highly impeachable during trials. One convict claiming to have heard another convict's admission of guilt is so common and so consistently spurious that lawyers routinely warn clients to be careful what they say around other inmates.

In Butch's case, such warnings were always futile.

The informant, whose statement was dated October 1987, claimed his information was unsolicited. However, his statement began with a request that a second sentence run concurrently with a first. He also wanted to serve his time in Pennsylvania where his wife was.

He said Butch had told him he had raped all the victims and decapitated one. He said Butch told him he had called NIS after the murders and, when they arrived, he was hugging a shotgun.

Butch later said the informant had encouraged him to talk,

and when he declined, had fabricated. But it would not have been surprising if Butch allowed, or even encouraged, fellow prisoners to believe he was a killer. To Butch, it may have been a way of adapting, a way of gaining a place in the prison pecking order. And he may have hoped a fearsome reputation would deter predatory older inmates from approaching him.

In addition to his reputation, Butch had other attributes one NIS agent thought might intimidate fellow inmates. The agent suggested that Butch's forbidding appearance, which attracted such negative attention during the 1981 investigation, would have served to protect him in jail.

"Off the bat, nobody in prison would want to screw with him, thinking he's killed three people," the agent suggested. "And looking at him, he's scary. If I was stopped at a stop sign and he pulled up next to me, I'd hit my automatic door lock and go for my gun."

But another inmate tells a different story. This man was briefly incarcerated with Butch in Nash County and later served several months in the Onslow County Jail while Butch was there.

Asked to describe his friendship with Butch, he said, "Me, Smith and Stevens gave one another cigarettes when the others ran out. People used to pick on him because he was so small and they knew he couldn't defend himself. And I felt like if I had a little brother in jail I would want someone to look out for him the same way." Butch never told him he killed anyone, the inmate said.

After his stay in Nash County, Butch was returned to Fayetteville, then taken to Onslow County. "I figured I was going to be living in every county jail in North Carolina," he said later.

A hearing on the motions to suppress Butch's confession and incriminating statements as well as to quash the indictment was held in Raleigh in October of 1987 before Judge W. Earl Britt.

It was the first time Francis described his relationship with Butch. According to Francis' testimony, the relationship was poor and included many instances when he struck Butch.

"I tried to treat all the kids equally, and I was brought up in a home that what's good for one is good for all," he said. "That's where a lot of our problems came about, because I tried not to give the defendant any more slack than what I gave my own children."

Francis also testified as to how Freeman had convinced him to cooperate in setting up an interview with Butch. It was reminiscent of the grand jury testimony.

"All that I had been aware of is that the victims had their throats slashed. Agent Freeman revealed to me that, on Butch's little sister, there was more than a throat slashing. That her body had been mutilated.

"He further revealed that Butch's case had been reviewed by a series of psychiatrists and they indicated they felt Butch had committed these crimes, and that it was quite possible, even probable, that he would kill again. And that it was quite probable that his next victim would be his mother."

The motion to dismiss the grand jury indictments was denied on December 3. The judge ordered the trial to begin 20 days from that date.

"I was flabbergasted," Cannon recalled. "I called the public defender and said, what do I do now? He told me not to waste time appealing, that I was not going to win, that I needed my time to prepare for trial. He was right. If the appeal had been thrown out, I'd have been in a heck of a mess. I'd been spending all my energy on motions and I hadn't made a lot of headway in building a case. But I couldn't have lived with myself if I hadn't appealed."

Cannon did succeed in getting a bit of breathing room, a one-week continuance that pushed the trial date past the Christmas holiday.

He and Renny drove to Raleigh on Christmas Eve. They conferred with federal public defender William Martin, scrambled through a whirlwind shopping trip, then raced back to work.

Cannon devoted Christmas morning to celebrating the holiday, then directed the rest of the day's energy to the trial. He worked straight through Christmas night, sorting through discovery material, organizing files and doing what was necessary to prepare himself to pick a jury.

Despite the tremendous press of time, Cannon could not bring himself to ask his secretary to sacrifice her own Christmas to help him.

On December 28, the news was exhilarating. "Lo and behold, the Fourth Circuit granted my motion to stay the trial. It was the happiest I'd been in a long time."

Cannon's barrage of requests for more discovery material prompted Bogdanos to reassure Butch's defense attorney that the prosecution was not poised to pull rabbits from hats in the courtroom.

"If I have it, you have it," Bogdanos insisted.

On February 2, 1988, exactly one year after the first oral arguments in the case, Cannon faced the same panel of appellate judges. Harrison L. Winter was chief judge.

Cannon argued that the prosecution's dropping the juvenile charge violated both *ex post facto* and due process. It also represented vindictiveness and harassment on the part of the prosecution, the defense contended.

The court would not reach a decision until five months later. Meanwhile, in March, Cannon tried to get Butch released on bail. It was during the detention hearing, presided over by Britt, that the unmendable rift between Special Agent Michael Paul and NIS went on the record.

Cannon knew from Paul's previous testimony that the agent did not believe Butch was guilty and subpoenaed him for the hearing. As a witness for the defense, Paul, who was then special agent in charge for the polygraph unit at NIS headquarters in Washington, D.C., had moved into the ranks of the enemy.

When he went to the NIS disburser for a travel allowance, he was told that because he was appearing for the defense, NIS would not pay his expenses.

"I've been subpoenaed. My testimony is based on my performance as a NIS agent. I have to go," Paul protested.

The disbursing agent did not relent.

The U.S. Marshal Service disburser also hesitated to provide plane fare for a defense witness, according to Paul. But Paul was adamant and, after some discussion, the service agreed to pay his fare – one way. After the hearing, Cannon asked the judge to order the U.S. Marshal Service to pay Paul's return fare. The judge did so.

This hearing was the first time an agent went on record using the expression "tunnel vision" to describe the investigation. During this hearing, Cannon drew comparisons between the triple slaying at Camp Lejeune and the triple slaying at Fort Bragg for which Army Capt. Jeffrey McDonald was convicted. According to Cannon, Butch suffered by comparison.

"I point out there are probably more dissimilarities between this case and that case than there are similarities," Cannon contended. "One major dissimilarity is that in this particular situation, this young man is a juvenile and he's incarcerated. That defendant was free on bond for several years while the case was coming to trial."

The court was not moved. Britt ordered that Butch remain in jail.

But in July, the Fourth Circuit Court of Appeals handed Cannon a victory.

The judges ruled that once the government moved against Butch under one statute, charging him as a juvenile, it could not proceed against him under another by indicting him as an adult.

Bogdanos was bitterly disappointed.

"I wanted to appeal to the Supreme Court, but the solicitor general's office, who must approve government appeals, would not let us appeal because the case lacked precedent value. I thought it was a reasonable decision although I argued against it. There are just so many appeals that can be heard."

But Bogdanos did not regret his decision to prosecute. "I'm not a knee-jerk prosecutor. I did it in as fair and conscientious a manner as I could, based on all the evidence I saw."

More than two years after his arrest, it seemed, once again, that Butch was to be freed. The public, aware that Butch had confessed but unaware of the eyewitness and other exculpatory evidence, clearly had the impression that he was getting away with murder thrice over. The pressure to bring him to trial was fierce. And some in the legal community began considering yet another approach. Perhaps the state could succeed where the federal government had failed.

On the same day Butch was scheduled to be released, he was rearrested, this time by the state of North Carolina.

CHAPTER 23

STATE OF N.C. VS. BUTCH SMITH

Camp Lejeune, the most populous Marine base, is a showplace for the Corps. Its industrial and operational areas reveal appropriate spit-and-polish.

The base is also a model of environmental management. Threatened species such as alligators, bluebirds and red-cockaded woodpeckers are encouraged to thrive within its thousands of picturesque acres.

For the most part, Camp Lejeune's presence in Onslow County has been an asset. The base employs hundreds of civilians. Forty thousand Marines and sailors as well as their accompanying families support many civilian businesses in Jacksonville. Less-appreciative residents sometimes add that those businesses are largely fast-food restaurants, pawn shops and used car lots.

Many military personnel and civil servants retire near Lejeune to take advantage of commissary, post exchange and medical facilities. They and their guests also enjoy a resort's recreational amenities, including beautiful private beaches, marinas, stables, a bowling alley and golf course.

Older residents, descendants of the county's former planter-aristocracy, are not all so enthusiastic about the base's influence. They refer to Lejeune's establishment as "the invasion of 1941."

Where once were modestly gracious family homes are bars whose signs identify them as topless (sic). Where once were dense forests of long leaf pine are tattoo parlors and trailer parks.

But cooperation prevails, especially between civilian and military law enforcement agencies. Military personnel charged with crimes committed off-base may be turned over to military authorities for prosecution.

This frequently happens in the case of serious crimes. The civilian community, for the most part, welcomes the military's assumption of such prosecutions. It saves the state the cost of a trial and allows the military to bear responsibility for those it has brought into the state. It also assures that, in the case of conviction, the criminal will actually serve his sentence. Restrictions on overcrowded North Carolina prisons have resulted in criminals typically serving only a fraction of their sentences. In federal prison, the catch-phrase is: What you get is what you get.

Although it is common for the feds to assume authority over a service member apprehended off-base, it is unheard-of for the shift-of-authority to move the other way.

Because of routine interactions between base and civilian legal officials, it was to be expected that Bill Andrews, district attorney for the 4th Prosecutorial District, would have contact with Marine Captain and Special Assistant U.S. Attorney Bogdanos. But, Bogdanos said, he did not discuss the outcome of the Butch Smith case with Andrews. "As far as I was concerned, Butch Smith was going to be walking the streets," he said.

Andrews, a Duplin County native, exemplifies the courtly manners traditionally attributed to educated Southerners. From his offices in Onslow County, he had followed news of the 1981 triple homicide at Camp Lejeune with interest. His interest, however, had not included any inkling that he would be professionally involved in the case.

"Neither before nor since have I prosecuted any criminal cases on base," Andrews said in a 1993 interview. "What I knew in 1981 was what I heard in the media."

After the 4th Circuit Court of Appeals dismissed the indictment against Butch, John Bruce, head of the Criminal Division of the U.S. Attorney's Office for the Eastern District of North Carolina, contacted Andrews.

"He wanted to know if I thought there was any way North Carolina could prosecute," Andrews said.

It might seem that question had been settled in 1981. A letter from then N.C. Assistant District Attorney Joseph E. Stroud, dated the day of the murders, replied to a phone call from Assistant U.S. Attorney Wallace Dixon. In the letter, Stroud told Dixon, "it has always been my understanding that criminal offenses occurring on the Marine Corps installations in Onslow County fall exclusively within the federal jurisdiction. Even assuming concurrent jurisdiction exists, we will defer to cognizant federal authorities in this case."

The letter was significant because the state was about to reverse itself.

Andrews, who was Stroud's boss in 1981, agreed there had always been a presumption that the feds had exclusive jurisdiction at Camp Lejeune. But he did not feel federal prosecutors were steering him into particularly treacherous legal seas.

"The feds had the same interest I did, to see justice done. They felt there was evidence from which a jury could – and would – convict this man. The feds had struck out on purely technical grounds and, in a nutshell, could do nothing with him."

Andrews does not think federal prosecutors might have been wiser to try Butch as a juvenile in 1986.

"I honestly think they did the best they could. In '86, if they'd prosecuted him as a juvenile, the effect would have been: They try him. And the court says, you're guilty and you can go. Butch was nearly 21 then, so prosecutors would have been spinning their wheels."

Andrews began researching the possibility of trying the case at the state level. As part of his research he also reviewed material forwarded to him by federal prosecutors.

His decision to indict Butch in the state court was based on his conclusion that, although the state of North Carolina had, in 1941, ceded exclusive jurisdiction on base, there was no specific mention of juvenile matters.

The federal juvenile law that was in effect at the time "indicated a preference by the federal courts for state courts to handle juvenile matters. The feds will only handle juvenile matters the state can't or won't handle," Andrews concluded. He became more convinced the state might well have jurisdiction to try Butch.

On December 13, 1988, Butch was indicted in Onslow County for the three murders. He entered a plea of not guilty.

Bogdanos later said he was shocked to learn the state had picked up the case.

"Bill and I never discussed what would happen if the federal case failed. I didn't believe it would. It would have been incredibly dishonest of me to make the argument that the feds had jurisdiction then say, oh, never mind, the state can try him."

Even without complicity about what direction the case might take, Andrews and Bogdanos were certainly of one mind. Butch was guilty and must be brought to trial.

At this legal juncture another lawyer entered the fray on Butch's side.

Jacksonville attorney Chuck Henry was going into the county courthouse when he learned he'd been appointed to a murder case. He thought he was merely filling the gap until a Greenville attorney named Cannon took over.

Henry had attended The University of North Carolina at Chapel Hill and graduated from Wake Forest Law School in Winston-Salem a couple of years after Andrews. He had worked for Andrews as an assistant district attorney until lured into private practice.

182

His years in North Carolina had lent a southern patina to the New Jersey native's speech and demeanor. A tenacious workaholic, Henry appeared both boyish and bookish. But he could be creatively brash in the courtroom.

Henry spoke to Butch at the Onslow County jail, where he'd been brought from Fayetteville the night before, one week after the grand jury had indicted him.

"I introduced myself, but intentionally did not ask about the case. I was confident that Cannon would be taking over and just wanted to advise Butch not to talk. I wanted to warn him that other prisoners might try to use him in their plea bargains."

Getting Butch not to talk was a difficulty that would plague his lawyers. Henry was unaware that Butch had already been interviewed twice at the jail. The first interview, conducted by one SBI agent and one NIS agent, took place the night Butch arrived from Fayetteville.

During the interview, Butch vented years of frustration. His angry, rather incoherent hand-written statement includes the wrong date, December 23 instead of December 13. It is filled with increasing venom, directed at Freeman for double-crossing him and at Tyler for mistreating Connie then trying to get Butch in trouble.

He claimed to have "whipped Tyler's ass" three times the day before the murders. The third time, Butch wrote, Sharon intervened by asking, "What's the problem?"

The statement is disturbing. It is clear Butch thought he may have committed the crimes. But he struggles to explain to himself why he cannot remember.

"If I did do this, I deserve to die," he wrote in his statement. "I'm not cold-blooded. I have a conscience. You guys are doing what you have to do. I was terrified because of the void. I couldn't remember what I did, so I'd lie, say anything, to save my ass. There are big doubts in my head as to my innocence or guilt."

He said he felt responsible because he'd always claimed he checked to see all the doors were locked but they might not have been.

The record does not show what, if any, comments or questions interrogators were offering before or while Butch wrote.

The second interview took place early the following morning and included an additional agent and a sheriff's deputy. The interview skirted a fine legal edge.

"It was the same morning the federal charges were dismissed," Henry later said. "But before they were dismissed according to the clock. Federal court opens at nine. He was interviewed at seven. So, theoretically, he still had federal counsel."

The interview took place between 7:50 and 8:10 a.m.

According to an agent's report, Butch was advised of his rights. However, that waiver was not included with discovery materials given to Henry.

An agent asked Butch if he thought he was guilty of first-degree murder.

Butch said no, he felt he was only guilty of second-degree murder because he thought someone must have put "PCP" or some other drug in the marijuana he smoked.

In other words, because of the "void," Butch thought that if he did commit the crimes, he must have been under the influence of a hallucinogen that caused him to forget committing them.

The agent told Butch he could see why he'd be angry enough to kill Tyler and Sharon, but couldn't understand what Connie had done to deserve her death. Butch said he'd thought about it for years and it had to be because he couldn't leave any witnesses.

Butch also reiterated his story about fighting with Tyler over Tyler's supposed sexual mistreatment of Connie. He told the agents he jumped on Tyler in the front yard and told him to leave Connie alone. He angrily told Tyler to screw his own sister and leave other people's sisters alone.

But, as in the case of his 1981 statements about getting out his shotgun the night of the killings, Butch may have been fabricating a scenario where he acted as the "macho" protector of his family.

CHAPTER 24

THE COURTS SUPREME

Butch had been in jail for three years by the time he arrived at the Onslow County jail. He was familiar with jail routine and, to Henry, seemed an average inmate. He didn't strike Henry as being particularly intimidating.

Henry talked to Cannon by phone within a day or two. He was surprised by the self-effacing Cannon's limited trial experience.

"But I knew he must have done some great legal work for the case to get thrown out of federal court," Henry said.

Cannon told Henry he wanted his help. The all-consuming nature of the case was seriously straining Cannon's fledgling practice.

"I had four law partners and could afford to take the time off for research," Henry recalled. "Rick had to make a living."

Henry was won over, not so much by Cannon as by the case itself. "The more I knew of it, the more interested I

185

became. It whetted my appetite to get to the bottom of the case."

From the beginning, Henry knew the prosecution's case hinged on the confession. He felt the confession was an absurdity. But he knew the power even an absurd confession can exert on a jury.

"I predicted Andrews would put on evidence of the murders, the autopsies, the confession and then rest. He'd leave all the evidence stuff for me to introduce. He was going to simplify the case to: there were three horrible murders, he confessed, turn him loose if you want to. I knew the only way to represent Carlton was to prove his confession was false."

No simple task. It's rare for a case even to go to a jury if there is a confession.

"People who confess usually plead guilty to something," Henry said. "They don't contest it."

Henry's defense theory was novel – and perilous – enough to set most lawyers' teeth on edge.

"It could have been like walking through a minefield and blown up in my face. I would have needed Butch's permission to use it. I planned on shocking the jury by saying, when Butch Smith tells you on the witness stand that he didn't commit these murders, you can't believe him. When he tells you he did it, in his statements, in his confession, you can't believe him either."

Henry was determined to get the confession out of the picture and force the state to prove the case through objective and circumstantial evidence – something he believed they'd have trouble doing. He would reinforce his point with he glaring inconsistencies in the confession.

"They wanted the jury to believe, on one hand, that this kid was so brilliant he could pull this off and not leave any physical evidence. And yet his confession included naive rationalizations. Such as cleaning up blood with a red washcloth."

Andrews said he was not surprised nor deterred by inconsistencies in Butch's alleged confession.

"It would not be unusual for a perpetrator not to remember what he did or the way he did certain things. We all have done things and had difficulty reconstructing them. Like the situation where someone loses his car keys and can't remember where he left them."

How, then, does one separate a genuine confession from one made by a disturbed, but innocent, person?

"That's a factual question a court would have to resolve," Andrews said. "There were statements Butch made to officers and there was other incriminating evidence at the scene."

Andrews declined to specify what evidence he meant. "I was satisfied there was sufficient evidence. If I hadn't been, I wouldn't have proceeded."

Henry interviewed Butch repeatedly. And taped the interviews. He made several efforts to provoke Butch into an outburst of temper.

"I'd get right in his face and try to make him angry, trip him up like in a cross-examination. I wanted to see him lose control. But he'd always back down."

Henry realized early that Butch frequently lied. But he saw it as childish posturing and dismissed most of it.

"When I'd catch him in a discrepancy, he'd laugh, shrug his shoulders and go on."

"I have a problem shooting off my mouth," Butch told him. "I don't have to turn it on. It turns on by itself."

Butch could rarely pass up an opportunity to portray himself as more "macho" or knowledgeable than he really was. Even at the expense of the truth.

"I'm thinking about having an operation and having my vocal cords taken out," he wryly remarked.

But on one point he was consistent. "He always maintained his innocence," Henry said. "Never once did he slip."

Butch explained he had been willing to accept blame for the killings, reasoning that if so many people believed him to be guilty, he must be guilty. But if he had little difficulty convincing others he was guilty, he had a great deal of difficulty convincing himself.

"Every time I try to convince myself I'm guilty, there's something that sticks in the back of my mind and says, no way," Butch told Henry.

Like most defense attorneys, Henry was not obliged to endlessly brood over whether his client was guilty.

According to the law, the issue was not Butch's guilt. It was whether the state could prove that guilt.

Procedurally, the question was whether the state of North Carolina had the right try Butch at all.

Henry's research convinced him the state did not.

"Camp Lejeune is just like a foreign country," Henry concluded. "North Carolina had no more jurisdiction than if the murders had been in Virginia."

Andrews and Henry did agree that any question about jurisdiction needed to be settled before the start of what promised to be a lengthy, costly trial.

Henry filed the perfunctory motion to dismiss for lack of jurisdiction.

Superior Court Judge James R. Strickland denied the motion on February 23, 1989. But he allowed a stay in the proceedings so Henry would have time to ask the state Supreme Court for a *writ of certiorari.*

The state Supreme Court allowed the writ, meaning it agreed to review the issue of jurisdiction separate from other issues in the case.

"Ordinarily," Andrews explained, if a defendant loses on a motion before trial, he can't appeal until he's been convicted. But because this was a serious, complicated issue, Chuck and I joined in asking the court to review the issue."

The cases cited by the attorneys concerned such diverse situations as a woman who was assaulted in a post office and a cow hit by a train at Fort Leavenworth.

The prosecution supported the state's claim to jurisdiction with a case verbosely titled "Howard v. Commissioners of Sinking Fund of City of Louisville."

In this case, the civilian workers at a naval ordnance plant in downtown Louisville objected when the city annexed the land where the plant was located and tried to enforce an occupational tax on plant employees.

The court said the annexation was legal because a simple change in municipal borders didn't interfere with federal jurisdiction. A later federal law allowed the city to tax the employees' wages.

Henry felt because the Sinking Fund case didn't deal with criminal law, it wasn't applicable to the Smith case.

One of the more colorful cases cited by the defense concerned a man who killed another in a freight car parked in the right-of-way of a railroad that ran through Nebraska's Fort Robinson.

The defendant claimed that because the state of Nebraska had authority to repair the roads and railways that passed through the fort land, its authority would also extend to crimes committed within those rights-of-ways.

The court had disagreed. It ruled that the federal government's allowing the state to repair roads running through fort property did not allow the state to assume any other jurisdiction.

After hearing the arguments in the Butch Smith case, the N.C. Supreme Court ordered that the indictments against Butch be dismissed.

The decision, filed February 7, 1991, said the federal government had exclusive jurisdiction over crimes committed at Camp Lejeune.

The justices were well aware that they were thwarting the public will. And, perhaps, freeing a triple murderer.

In the decision, the court quoted former Chief Justice Stacy's remark concerning another North Carolina case, State v. DeBerry, 1945: "This may lead to an undesirable result. Nevertheless, we can only declare the law as we find it."

Judge Harry C. Martin concurred but for a different reason. In his statement, he explained how Butch Smith could have been brought to trial. According to the judge, there had, indeed, been a way by which a juvenile charged with committing a crime on federal land could have been tried as an adult.

He began by conceding there was an apparent gap in tate and federal jurisdiction in 1981.

"However, the Federal Assimilative Crimes Act cures this gap in the federal jurisdiction," Martin wrote.

The Federal Assimilative Crimes Act states that anyone

who commits an act on a federal reservation that is not punishable under federal law, but would be punishable in the state where the reservation is situated, can be found guilty of the state offense and similarly punished.

"The provisions of this Act have been in effect since 1825," Martin wrote. "It provides criminal laws for federal enclaves by use of the state law to fill gaps in federal criminal law."

In 1981, North Carolina law allowed a juvenile 14 years or older to be tried for murder as an adult.

By applying the Federal Assimilative Crimes Act, incorporating the state law into federal criminal law, the United States had jurisdiction to try Butch Smith for the capital charges of murder.

Because the federal government could have used this gap-closing procedure, the state of North Carolina could not claim jurisdiction.

Martin closed with a few scathing words for the prosecution. "Inexplicably, counsel and the court failed to recognize and apply the Federal Assimilative Crimes Act in deciding and reviewing the issue of whether this defendant could be tried as an adult in the federal court for these three murders.

"Had the federal court done so, these murder cases could have been adjudicated in 1987."

Bogdanos said there was an explainable reason why he had not proceeded under the Federal Assimilative Crimes Act.

"I didn't think it was applicable," he said. The act refers to crimes not punishable under federal law. There is, and was, a federal murder statute, Bogdanos said.

"In my mind, to have used the Federal Assimilative Crimes Act would have been dishonest because we would have been doing an end run – doing indirectly what we couldn't do directly."

Butch Smith was released March 15, 1991, having spent nearly five years in jail. He was greeted by reporters and the ever-loyal Mary Cheek, the mother of his friend, Tom.

Butch had only kind words for the Onslow County sheriff's department.

"The jailers were happy for him," Henry said. "They're good people. And Butch had been in their care longer than any other inmate."

Butch called Betty from Henry's office where he was eating pizza. Betty told her son she'd be at the airport in Buffalo when he arrived. She'd decided to forgo the stress of meeting Butch, and the press, at the jail.

Henry reassured her, "He's a big boy. He can get home all right."

Butch was free. But it was still not over.

Henry found out that the state planned to appeal to the U.S. Supreme Court.

This was to be preceded by application for a *writ of certiorari* similar to the one sought from the state Supreme Court. The basis of this writ was whether the N.C. Supreme Court had the authority to decide whether Camp Lejeune had jurisdiction over Butch. Was federal jurisdiction a matter that only could be decided in a federal court?

The case had come full circle. Having argued that the federal government could not dictate to the state, the state was now asking the court to say no one but a federal court could dictate!

Henry expected the matter to be denied out of hand. It was not.

"I got a call from the clerk of the Supreme Court on Wednesday. A very dignified voice said the chief justice wanted me to file a brief in opposition to the request for the writ. And he wanted it by noon Monday."

Henry told the clerk he wasn't licensed to practice in the Supreme Court. The clerk dryly remarked that Henry needn't worry about that.

"I believe Chief Justice Rehnquist can overlook that if he wishes," Henry was told.

"Monday at noon? Does Federal Express deliver to the Supreme Court by noon?" Henry sputtered.

"I suggest you take that up with them," the clerk replied.

Andrews was also surprised, albeit more pleasantly.

"Most cases that get to the Supreme Court by the route this

one took, the court summarily denies to hear. Nobody makes any arguments," Andrews said. "This time, they didn't summarily deny it."

Within days of the clerk's first call, the court asked Henry for another brief. Henry was stunned.

"The more they asked for, the more I thought, Oh, my God, they're going to hear it!"

Henry was terrified. And thrilled. And torn. It was a glorious opportunity.

"It's like the Super Bowl for lawyers," he explained. "But the best thing for Butch was that they deny the writ and let the state Supreme Court have the last word."

Henry finished the requested brief. And had it printed and professionally bound, in accordance with U.S. Supreme Court requirements, all at his own expense. The state does not reimburse expenses incurred by indigent cases beyond the state level.

On his expenses sheet Henry jotted, "Kiss $2,500 dollars good-by."

The purpose of the U.S. Supreme Court is not to correct mistakes made in lower courts. The court is not interested in the particular two parties in a case, but in what effect their case might have on society.

In the Butch Smith case, the only one affected was Butch Smith. The juvenile law which prosecutors contended allowed Butch to escape his just punishment had been changed.

The court denied the writ. There was no opinion.

"It was almost anti-climactic," Henry recalled. "It ended with the word 'denied' and the chief justice's initials."

But Henry would not tell Butch until he was absolutely sure. "I always had in the back of my mind they were going to do something else to him. I went to Andrews and said, 'Bill, this kid's been through a lot of disappointments. If there's anything else you're going to do, let me know. Don't let him walk out the jail door and then get served with another warrant.' "

"That's the end of it," Andrews said.

Henry suspects that deep down Andrews was relieved.

"The logistics of this case would have monopolized him

for four or five months. It was kind of like the dog that chases cars and finally catches one."

If Andrews did feel relief, it was diluted by grievous disappointment. He told reporters that the ruling was "probably the worst miscarriage of justice that I've seen in a really serious case in the 19 years that I've been prosecuting."

He remained convinced of Smith's guilt and disappointed in the outcome.

"I'm just sorry that the court didn't give us the opportunity to try him. It's a shame that those three people were killed and nobody's ever going to be tried for it."

The prosecutor's indignation was warranted if Butch was the killer. If not, an even greater indignation was warranted.

If Butch was not the killer, an innocent man spent five years in jail. A man beset by emotional problems rooted in a chaotic childhood was separated from the few people who loved him. He was subjected to the terror, loneliness and numbing boredom of imprisonment.

And an anonymous someone, who killed three people the night of August 24, 1981, had managed to put a decade of liberty between himself and the crimes.

CHAPTER 25

AFTERMATH

Chuck Henry drove Butch to the Jacksonville airport the day he was released. Butch was wearing a sweater Henry had given him and carrying a suitcase Henry had scrounged from his attic.

"You've got to remember, he had nothing," Henry said. "You leave jail with a garbage bag."

Henry had been prepared to pay Butch's airfare to New York if Betty hadn't been able to.

One female television reporter had followed Butch to the airport. "She forgot to ask him if he did it," Henry said derisively. He fielded her questions, allowing Butch to enter the terminal without being subjected to yet another interrogation.

At the ticket counter, Butch was asked to present some identification. He was released shortly after the end of the Persian Gulf War. During the war, airport officials had starting asking passengers for identification as part of check-in procedures, hoping to deter aspiring terrorists.

Henry explained to the ticket agent that the prospective passenger had no identification because he had spent the past five years in jail. The ticket agent looked at Butch more closely and registered uneasiness when he recognized the subject of so many gruesome newspaper stories. Butch stood passively by as the agent expressed reluctance to let him board the plane. Henry presented the agent with a much more threatening demeanor than his client. "I told him, 'Butch is getting on that plane if I have to fly it myself.'"

To reassure the nervous agent, Henry suggested airport officials take Butch into a back room "and strip-search him if necessary." After ascertaining that neither Butch nor his borrowed suitcase harbored any weapons, the agents allowed him to get on the plane.

As for Butch, his exhilaration at being free was tempered by a curious discomfort at suddenly being responsible for his own decisions. His spirits lifted considerably when his plane neared Buffalo, where his family was waiting.

"It was the longest ten minutes of my life," he recalled. "I couldn't wait to get on the ground."

He was met by his grandparents, Betty and Betty's friend, a genial farmer who would prove as loyal to Butch as he was to Butch's mother.

The group's first stop was to see Butch's newborn nephew, Lorrie's son.

"That was my top priority," Butch said.

But his adjustment to freedom was not immediate. He said that for weeks after his release, when the family would go out to dinner, he would become so disconcerted after 15 minutes or so that he would walk outside to regain his composure. The problem was that he felt overwhelmed in a situation where he was expected to make several decisions in a short time.

Another difficulty he faced was the notoriety he had gained during his years in prison. He knew that some people believed he had gotten away with murder.

In time, the discomfort associated with decision making would fade. And the notoriety would abate. But Butch would never be exonerated in the eyes of many, including some of his family.

Butch was not the only one involved in the Kentucky Court investigation who faced legal difficulties in the eighties.

Arnold Sleeper, NIS Special Agent in Charge at the time of the murders, was accused of misusing his authority in connection with a later, unrelated matter. An NIS internal investigation of a November 1982 incident resulted in Sleeper's being brought back to U.S. District Court in New Bern from Florida, where he had retired.

Early in 1985, two counts of embezzlement of public money were dismissed in exchange for Sleeper's plea of nolo contendere to one count of theft of personal property. The misdemeanor charges arose from Sleeper's having run out of money at a Jacksonville bar, where several NIS agents were unwinding after work. Sleeper asked a junior agent to lend him money. When the agent told his boss he had no money, Sleeper told the agent to give him the official money he carried to pay informants and make undercover drug buys. The agent hesitated, but when his superior insisted, he gave Sleeper $60.

That same night, Sleeper also borrowed $40 from another junior agent. The subsequent investigation concluded this was not official money. The next day, the first agent asked Sleeper to replace the official money, which he did. The second agent then approached Sleeper to be reimbursed and was told to take up a collection from the other agents who'd been in the bar.

By this time, Sleeper's autocratic attitude had earned him the animosity of more than two subordinates.

The charges and his sentence, which required Sleeper to repay the $40 in addition to a $450 fine, were not reported in local newspapers. But the events did not pass unnoticed.

"All the NIS agents knew Sleeper had been fried and humbled," reported an investigator. "It was the arrogance of the acts that rankled."

Sleeper returned to Florida where he died of cancer in early 1990.

Others concerned in the case have fared more favorably.

R. Reid Bogie, Marine special assistant in 1981, is in private practice in Brookfield, Conn. He intends to retire in North Carolina.

Matthew Bogdanos is assistant district attorney for New York City. He is a major in the Marine Corps Reserve, an amateur boxer and a Big Brother. He is still single and still keeps the material related to the Butch Smith case "memorialized" in his office.

Richard and Renny Cannon have had two sons since Butch's case was dismissed. On the weekends Cannon works, the pre-schoolers sometimes spend an hour or two tumbling around their father's office. Cannon is as unflappable about his children's antics as he is about the antics of a legal adversary.

Cannon is still in private practice in Greenville and still active in the Jaycees. The organization honored him with their Distinguished Service Award in 1992.

Chuck Henry also remains in private practice in Jacksonville. He and his wife have had a daughter since the Smith case made its final charge through the court system.

Henry assumed much of the responsibility, and initial headaches, of starting a chapter of the Boys and Girls Club in Onslow County. He spends nearly as much time touting fund-raisers for the group as he does touting clients' innocence.

Lorrie is married and the mother of a toddler son whom Betty adores. She never has been able to fully dispel the horrors of 1981. Betty said it is difficult for her son-in-law and many others to understand why the family cannot simply put the traumatic events in the past.

Butch lives with his mother in the house she has bought. Betty said she wishes she had the baby shoes, family photos and other personal items NIS seized during the investigation and never returned. She has no plans to marry, but the genial farmer is a special friend. Betty is very fond of him, as are Lorrie and Butch.

"He's a big man, looks like a lumberjack, but he's one of the kindest people you'd ever want to meet," Betty said. "He's gone out of his way for my kids and asked nothing in return. He's my best friend."

Butch is a volunteer fireman and has worked as a ski-lift operator. In the summer, he works as a laborer on a tree farm. He now has a driver's license.

Asked what he would like his life to be five years down the road, Butch said, "I want to be left alone. I want this to be solved so my mom and I can go on with our lives."

His dream vocation is to be a civil engineer who works mostly outdoors.

"I can't picture myself behind a counter or a desk," he said. For now, Betty said, Butch generally prefers to stay close to home, visiting his sister and grandparents and occasionally going out with a friend for a game of pool.

Connie Smith, Sharon Sager and Tyler Dash are buried next to each other. Betty tends to the grave sites. It was she who paid a bit each week to buy Connie and Sharon's gravestones.

Neither Betty nor her parents have seen Sharon's two youngest children since her death. Debbie Dash visits her grandparents but not Betty.

Betty is a licensed practical nurse. For now, she has no plans to become a registered nurse, as she was in the state of North Carolina. She thoroughly enjoys her job at a nursing home. Betty said she prefers working with the elderly because when they die there is the consolation that they lived a full life.

She continues to grieve for Connie and yearns for a clear-cut resolution of the events of August 24, 1981.

Betty said that she agreed to be interviewed in connection with this book, despite the risk of being again subjected to public judgment, for one reason only. She desperately hopes that someone who can definitively explain who and why will take the burden from her family.

"We can't put this to rest," Betty said, "because we can't blame something, a heart attack, an illness. We have no one to blame either because if we blame who they tell us to blame, we've got even more grief."

CHAPTER 26

EPILOGUE

With few exceptions, investigators interviewed for this book were convinced of Butch's guilt. But that conviction usually was based on incomplete information or misinformation. One NIS agent was unaware that someone in the apartment, Bobby Davis, claimed to have seen Sharon Sager killed. Another had been told that Bobby's statements were dubious because he only recalled the murder while under hypnosis. And another agent, who'd seen the composite drawings of a bearded suspect, was surprised to learn of the beard hairs found on the towel with Tyler's blood.

One investigator passed on the view that the confession matched the crime scene "in every detail." When asked about the apparent discrepancies between the descriptions of the wounds in the autopsy reports and the confession, the agent was more willing to speculate that the medical examiner had erred than to speculate that Butch was innocent.

For most of the investigators, it seemed to boil down to a matter of statistical odds. A young man with a history of violent outbursts is at the scene of a violent crime. What were the odds that another person with the potential for violence also had been in the house that night?

But there are other odds to consider. What are the odds that a witness would describe the killer as having a beard, that beard hairs would be found on a bloody towel and yet the killer actually be a beardless boy?

What are the odds that an unidentified bloodstain, found near drops of a victim's blood, would belong to someone other than the killer? Isn't it more likely that the killer inadvertently cut himself while stabbing his victims?

What are the odds that an unidentified bloody palm print, found near a victim's body, would belong to someone other than the killer?

What are the odds that a typically sloppy teenager could so thoroughly clean up after three murders that investigators found no evidence to tie him to the crimes?

What are the odds that Butch was able to walk unseen to the woods and back through a densely populated residential area at 6:00 on a Monday morning? Is it more likely that the killer was able to arrive and leave by car without being seen?

What are the odds that a teenager repeatedly would catch two of his cousins having sexual relations but four other teenagers in the same house would see nothing?

Doubts about Butch's innocence linger because it is difficult for anyone reading his statements to understand why, if he were innocent, he could be so easily cajoled into such incriminating remarks. Agent Mike Paul suggested that to a boy like Butch, any attention was valuable – and exciting.

"He's an adolescent boy, sort of on-his-own. All of a sudden he's the center of attention in a homicide investigation. He was the hottest thing in North Carolina at the time. I'm sure he'd conjure up anything to keep this thing going."

But there may be another reason he sometimes seemed unsure of his innocence. Butch, lacking confidence in his own judgment and faced with an array of male authority figures, could not understand why they were so convinced he was guilty unless he was.

If he did not remember an event, he began to assume it was because his memory was faulty, not because he was being baited with inaccurate information. Repeatedly, Butch took the bait and accepted an agent's incriminating explanation for something, like the cut he had on his face the morning of the killings, which agents contended he got from one of the victims. He was unaware that Tommy Sager already had explained the cut as the result of an accident.

Could the defense have convinced a jury that Kraagman or someone else was a more credible suspect than Butch? Chuck Henry thinks not.

"The law allows the defense to produce evidence that someone else committed the murder. But he must show not only that the suspect had the opportunity, but must present enough evidence to indicate he really did it. You can't just speculate, well, so-and-so was in the house so they did it."

But there have been instances when the courts ruled that excluding evidence implicating another deprived the defendant of his constitutional rights.

Betty said a gruesome rumor sprang up in Springville after the victims' funeral that NIS had taken away the bodies secretly to preserve them as evidence. The rumor was nonsense. But the preservation of other evidence could be the key to identifying the killer.

Since 1981, there have been extraordinary innovations in forensic science. The most promising is DNA technology, often referred to as "chemical fingerprinting." The importance of DNA to criminal investigations is reflected in the fact that 90 percent of FBI laboratory research funds are earmarked for DNA.

The technology relies on the genetic coding unique to every person – except identical twins. The DNA code may be read from a blood or tissue sample many years old, if the sample has been properly preserved.

If DNA studies revealed that the unidentified blood stain found at the crime scene and root tissue from the mysterious "forcibly-removed" beard hair came from the same source, it would clearly indicate that someone other than Butch killed three people at Kentucky Court on the morning of August 24, 1981.

Odds are that the case will not be solved unless someone confesses and corroborates that confession with details that explain the evidence more plausibly than Butch was able to do.